HIDDEN RIFT WITH GOD

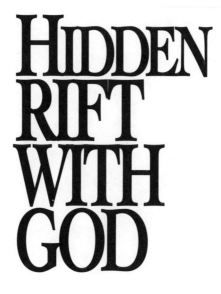

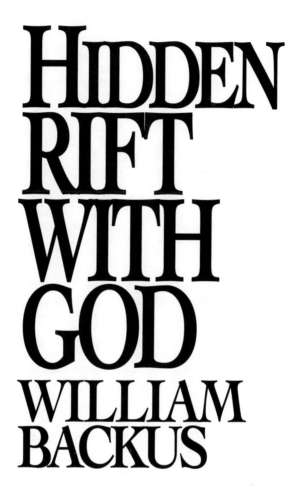

HIDDEN RIFT WITH GOD

WILLIAM BACKUS

BETHANY HOUSE PUBLISHERS
MINNEAPOLIS, MINNESOTA 55438

Published by Bethany House Publishers
A Ministry of Bethany Fellowship, Inc.
6820 Auto Club Road, Minneapolis, Minnesota 55438

Printed in the United States of America

Library of Congress Cataloging-in-Publication Data

Backus, William D.
    The hidden rift with God / William Backus.
        p. cm.

    I. Spiritual life. W. Theodicy. 3. Backus, William D.
I. Title.
BV4501.2.B249   1990
231'.8—dc20   90–34256
ISBN 1–55661–097–1   CIP

To Ed Wessling,

my old friend,

whose rift with God

has been healed.

Books by Dr. Backus

Finding the Freedom of Self-Control
Finding the Freedom of Self-Control Study Guide
    (with Steven Wiese)
The Hidden Rift With God
The Paranoid Prophet
Telling Each Other the Truth
Telling the Truth to Troubled People
Telling Yourself the Truth (with Marie Chapian)
Telling Yourself the Truth Study Guide
    (with Marie Chapian)
Untwisting Twisted Relationships
    (with Candace Backus)
Untwisting Twisted Relationships Study Guide
    (with Candace Backus)
What Did I Do Wrong? What Can I Do Now?
    (with Candace Backus)
Why Do I Do What I Don't Want to Do?
    (with Marie Chapian)

Tapes by Dr. Backus

Taking Charge of Your Emotions
Telling Each Other the Truth
Telling Yourself the Truth

WILLIAM BACKUS, Ph.D., is a Christian psychologist and an ordained Lutheran clergyman. He is Founder and Director of the Center for Christian Psychological Services in St. Paul, Minnesota. He and his family make their home in Forest Lake, Minnesota. He is also associate pastor of a large Lutheran church.

The Center for Christian Psychological Services receives numerous requests for referrals to licensed Christian professional counselors who use Christian cognitive therapy as set forth in Dr. Backus' books. The Center would be happy to receive from you a brief summary of your counseling experience with misbelief therapy and your qualifications, license status, and commitment to Christian truth in your practice. On the basis of such information, the Center will refer callers from your area to you. Please include a telephone number with area code, address, and the name of the facility with which you are affiliated.

The Center for Christian Psychological Services
Roseville Professional Center #435
2233 N. Hamline
St. Paul, Minnesota, 55113
(612) 633–5290

A Note from the Author

This book, like others I have written, contains numerous examples presented as clinical cases. Some readers are acquainted with a person who has been a patient of mine, while others have themselves seen me for treatment. So some may be tempted to find themselves, their friends, or their relatives in one or the other of these stories. The fact is that I do not publish actual, recognizable patient histories as examples. To me that is a breach of confidentiality. Instead, the stories are composites. Details have been deliberately altered, and actual histories have been blended. The stories are true in that they represent actual clinical phenomena. But they are not histories of any one particular client. If some of the symptoms appear to be your own, it is because many people experience difficulties having some similarity to one another.

Individuals described from non-clinical contexts are sometimes actual persons, while some are fictional.

Contents

An Urgent Word to the Reader

I am writing about two kinds of rifts. And since they wind together to form the whole of this book, it will help if I clearly identify these double strands at the outset.

The primary theme I'm addressing is the rift between man and God. I write to those who feel confused, disappointed, resentful and even angry with God. I write to those who cannot understand why they long for the very things that God has forbidden. And so, somewhere at the very depths of their soul lies a gaping chasm, separating them from God and from the happiness, peace and love they crave. Unable to see why they've been "dealt" their particular circumstances or desires, each of these folks winds up in a major rift with God.

My colleague, Irene Gifford was one who struggled painfully with just such a rift. Her circumstances may be more painful and extreme than your own—but I'll let her relate the experiences that carried her to the edge of her own inner rift.

Paul and I were richly blessed. We lived in a "gathering-in" kind of house, nestled under huge trees in a yard big enough in which to grow much of our own food. We had found it on our first wedding anniversary.

Our three children were a joy, passing with hardly a ripple through adolescence into young adulthood. By the time we had one at college, one in seminary, and one married and living less than a mile away, we had found fulfilling niches in our own professions. Paul worked at a nearby university, designing research equipment. He was truly gifted in his calling. I was a psychologist, preparing at the same time for ordination in the Episcopal church.

In the late afternoon, I looked forward to seeing his blue van pull into the driveway. That was my signal to start the vegetables cooking. He would make the salad while I put the finishing touches on dinner. Our lives slid into a comfortable, happy rhythm.

A big part of my own inner rhythm was based on the love and support of this wonderfully caring man. He *always* took care of us. He was never sick, always strong. And then, my world upended.

First, the diagnosis: Paul had a serious heart ailment. He went into an unusual depression.

A month later, Paul shot himself, and my life was torn apart. Compounding the shock and grief, his ashes were stolen in a church burglary.

Even while being loved and reassured by family, neighbors and my extended parish family, I tortured myself with guilt. Why had I gone to church that morning when Paul hadn't felt up to it? I was a psychologist—why hadn't I been aware that he was suicidal? I hadn't even been able to help my own husband.

After a time, however, my agonizing guilt gave way to anger at God. How had He let this happen? Why? Paul didn't deserve the illness, or the depression. My children didn't deserve to lose their father, nor I my husband. What kind of a "heavenly Father" would treat His children so cruelly?

We'd prayed so earnestly together for his healing. Our family, and friends—even friends of friends from all over the world—had prayed, too.

But God had not touched my husband. He had not worked through the doctors. I learned that even the medication had been wrong. *Everything* had gone wrong.

Even while I was being nourished and upheld by God in my grief, I wrestled with Him. The pain seemed too great to bear. I prayed less, because God seemed indifferent to me. During the struggle that ensued I wrote the poem about Martha on page 34.

Searching the Scriptures, I realized that Martha was not my only companion in this keen sorrow, pain, disappointment and *perhaps even anger* at God. There were many others.

Job acknowledged such a rift (Job 7:17–21). The psalmist owned up to it (Psalm 73:13). Jeremiah admitted it (Jeremiah 20:7), and so did Naomi (Ruth 1:20).

But looking in the Bible, I found, was only the beginning of my journey back to the side of God. It also required long, prayerful looks inside myself at the rift that *I* had allowed to come between God and me. After a long way, after a long time, I once again began to sense the presence of Christ at my side— to understand (as only He can help *anyone* understand) that He never had been far from me, never had been against me, though I'd accused Him of that and more.

It was only after much inner work and finding the right path to healing for my inner ache that God's promise through Isaiah became *real* to me: " 'For a brief moment . . . I hid my face from you, but with everlasting kindness I will have compassion on you,' says the Lord, your Redeemer" (54:8).

Only by undertaking the inner journey—beyond denial, then beyond sorrow and anger—can anyone begin to close the rift with God.

Something of my experience is reflected in the poems between the chapters of this book. They are written, in part, about a canoe trip our family took the summer after Paul's death; a canoe trip we had always before taken with Paul.

There are others I want to address, those who haven't suffered the kind of circumstances that Irene has gone through. I'm speaking of men and women who disagree with God about right and wrong—those who cannot understand why God still waves His "antiquated" laws in our faces when the world has moved on to a "freer, easier" approach to life.

At the root of it all—whether wrestling with circumstances, or wanting to live without limits—lies the same problem: a hidden rift with God.

This book is primarily addressed to those who have suffered from this spiritual malady—and malady it is—and are ready to put an end to the confusion it's wreaking in their lives.

I said that this book would address not only two kinds of people but two kinds of rifts. The second rift is the one between modern psychology and Christianity. That there is a rift here at all is, in my thinking, too bad.

Here is one side of this rift: Secular psychologists analyze human problems in terms of *material* cause and effect. If you lose your temper and yell at your family, it must be due to your upbringing or to pre-menstrual syndrome. If you kill two people, it must be that you're deranged because of vicious childhood experiences. If you molest children repeatedly, your behavior must be due to "sexual addiction." There is some truth in these formulations, as far as they go. But they ignore spiritual and moral considerations. This materialistic myopia riddles psychological theory and practice to the point where a thoughtful person, who has considered spiritual and moral issues, may feel compelled to choose either psychology or religion.

On the other side of the psychology/religion rift stand some well-intentioned Christian writers whose books have denounced "Christian psychology." This has not helped to bridge the gap—though bridge it we must, because there *is* truth on both sides.

The Bible teaches truth about man's psychology; you cannot deny this if you understand that the word *psychology* means "knowledge about the soul or mind." Given this understanding of psychology, it's quite true to say that a biblical psychology existed long before contemporary psychology came into being. Christian theology has something to say, both to the person practicing psychological therapies and to the client who receives counseling.

According to Christian teaching, you cannot deal with deviant human behavior as if man is a malfunctioning computer. There are realities which, though invisible, exert real and powerful influences on human behavior—for instance, a universal and inborn inclination to do wrong (as it is defined by God's command), the existence of potent, evil, spiritual entities, and the presence and activity of God's Holy Spirit.

In effect, psychology and Christian theology span, or attempt to span, the same gulf, because both deal with human behavior and its ills. I have worked for twenty-five years to understand how the insights from both fields fit together. Many problems are involved. One major difficulty is sectarianism in both fields. So many competing theories of human behavior and treatment exist, each with its own convinced adherents, that there is no way to explore how each relates to Christian teaching. And the divisions among Christian theologians are as plenteous as the splits among secular psychologists. No one can claim to speak for all the systems of psychotherapy or for every school of Christian thought.

Because of the disagreements, and because of the variety of positions, I believe readers are entitled to a straightforward summary of an author's orientation on psychological *and* spiritual matters. So I want to tell you right off where I'm coming from.

Theologically, my background is evangelical, conservative and biblical. To me, as a confessional Lutheran, the Word of God is absolute truth, though no human being can rightly claim to know all truth absolutely. As a psychologist, I write from a cognitive behavioral perspective, chosen partly because it is readily modified by and subordinated to Christian truth. In relation to the truth of Scripture, cognitive psychology is merely a method of understanding how the human mind works to process material, including the material offered by Scripture.

I have deliberately related certain biblical terms to psychological equivalents. Sometimes, however, the psychological must be moved over to accommodate the prior claims of God's revealed truth. For instance, the fundamental human plight is not anxiety or the oedipal situation or imbalance in neurotransmitting chemistry, though all of these may exist. Man's greatest plight is a separation from his Source, which is God. This separation was wrought by human sin. Sin, at its core, is fed by untruth stated and restated in the internal monologue, the thoughts of the heart and mind of man. We alienate ourselves from God by actively contradicting Him, by taking issue with Him over what is good. Instead of accepting His view of what is good for us, we disagree with Him; we wish for and act on our own view of what is good.

The cure is not insight, or desensitization, or healing of memories, or making the unconscious conscious, or increased rationality, or finding one's real self, though one or another of these may help. The cure is God's free gift of righteousness, gained for us when Jesus offered himself for us. We gain this gift by grace through faith. This righteousness alone reunites us with God; it is our life-giving reconnection to our Source. Faith is built by stating and restating the truth in the self-talk—in other words, telling yourself the truth. Both righteousness and faith come from God, not from our own efforts. It is the *living out* of both righteousness and faith that requires energetic commitment and effort.

And so this brings me, at last, to my reason for the title of this opening piece, "An Urgent Word . . ." Though this is not a "ten-steps-to-wholeness" book, it is intended to be a volume that will help you find inner wholeness—which is peace with God at the deepest level. And the reason I wanted you to read this first is that you must know: A counselor or writer can help you discover the pathway; but you must take yourself step-by-step to the goal. The *work* is up to you.

Understanding that, by all means proceed.

Fragments

When he died so violently
    in his despair,
he shattered my heart as well,
And all the pieces of my life
lie scattered in bruised fragments
    at my feet.
I will gather up the fragments
    one by one,
        and ponder them
To see if there be any form or continuity;
    to look for tracings of God
        to fit my life together
            once again.

How the Lord in his anger
has set the daughter of Zion
    under a cloud.

The Lord has become like an enemy,
    He has destroyed Israel.

ONE

Running From the One Who Loves Us

Jack awoke to a stinking and bitter cold apartment. During the party someone had smashed a window, but that hardly mattered because the heat had been turned off last week. His last bit of money went to buy the "crack" and tequila and some cheap pot that fueled last night's blowout.

When he tried to stand, his head felt as if someone had split it with an ax. The reek of stale cigarette smoke caught him and he had to stagger into the bathroom where he bent double, retching.

As he splashed cold water on his face, Jack remembered: This was the "day of reckoning." Jack's two roommates had split three days ago, taking his stereo and anything else he might have hocked to cover the two months' back rent they owed. He'd "borrowed" so much money from his girlfriend that she'd finally told him to take a flying leap off a bridge. He had to get out of here before the landlord showed up. Or the police. Life was as bitter as the taste in his mouth.

He scraped the cold razor over his face, then stuffed jeans and a sweatshirt into his gym bag. There was only one place left to go. One person left to turn to.

It was four days of hitchhiking and rifling McDonald's dumpsters for food—then a three-mile walk down the dirt road. At last, the familiar board fence was in sight. There was the house, with the maple tree he used to climb. Someone was out in the yard, raking.

As Jack turned down the gravel drive, the man beneath the maple tree lifted his head, hesitating only a moment. Then he dropped the rake and rushed toward Jack, his face beaming, his eyes glistening with sudden tears.

Jack found himself wrapped in that bear hug he hadn't felt since he left home in anger four years before. Burying his face in Jack's hair, his father whispered, "I've been praying you'd come home."

Jack stiffened and pulled away. "I just need a place to crash. I need some money—that's all—and I'll be on my way."

Patiently his father replied, "Why don't we just wait awhile before we talk about that. Come inside and rest. Mom's got a big roast in the freezer. Once you eat and get some sleep we'll talk. What d'ya say?"

"I want one thing clear from the beginning," Jack said coldly. "I know there are still some bonds with my name on them. That's *all* I'm here for. Not to discuss my life-style—and not to hear a sermon. You and Mom have your ideas, and I have mine. I'm not staying here any longer than I have to. This may be your idea of a 'good life,' but I don't want to live in a re-run of *Little House on the Prairie*. Okay?"

As they climbed the back steps to the kitchen door, his father gently laid a hand on Jack's shoulder. "All right, Son. You're welcome to stay as long as you like. The bass are biting over in the pond. Maybe we can do a little fishing—just talk, like we used to do."

Jack jerked the hand off his shoulder. "I'm *not* interested. I told you when I left—I don't need your *talk*. And I don't need you. I just want what's mine. And I want to live my own life—*my* way . . ."

Jack's story may sound harsh and bitter to you. Maybe it's difficult for you to relate to him. Unfortunately, it's a story that is probably true of almost every one of us at one time or another, spiritually speaking. Undoubtedly, you recognize it as a new twist on an old parable, and it was written to illustrate the way we often treat the one person who truly wants what's best for us all the time. That, of course, is our heavenly Father.

Like Jack, many of us suffer pain that's partly because of other people, partly because life seems determined to give us a battering, and—if we ever get honest—partly of our own making. There are others of us, however, *unlike* Jack, who did absolutely nothing to cause or to deserve the pain that winds itself around us, like a cord cutting into our souls. Maybe you go through your days and many empty nights wondering what you did to deserve this *hurt, grief, loneliness, alienation,* or desperate sense that *life is meaningless.*

Whether this pain is of your own making or not, there is almost always a deeper feeling that is masked by the others. Beneath the pain or numbness lies a force that wants to lash out and hurt the thing that hurt us—an animal reflex anger.

This reflex can save your life—if you're an animal. When a trap's steel jaws snap through flesh and bone, an animal will normally react instantly. Frenzied with pain, it lunges again and again, tearing at the trap and at its own leg, trying to stop the pain and get free. Sometimes the animal actually gets itself free, but its own extreme behavior causes it to bleed to death in the end.

Many of us achieve the same kind of ironic "success." Thinking that our reflexive anger is *saving* us from pain, it actually becomes that force which, left to itself, causes us to bleed to death slowly, emotionally and spiritually speaking.

The greater irony (and greater sorrow) is that when the one big hand that *can* set us free from our particular pain offers to do so, we react by biting it. We behave as if the rift we feel between ourselves and God is *His* fault. We reject Him and His love the way "Jack" rejected his father—and we do so to our own detriment.

I know. There was a time when circumstances clamped shut on the tender and good things in my own life. Pain filled me up, blinded me, and I vented my anger on the very One who had the power to shield me from pain. Wasn't He ultimately responsible? Even if, as the Bible teaches, He's the great healer—wasn't He ultimately responsible for the fact that I had pain at all?

To me, our family looked like everybody's dream. My wife and I had four charming, well-behaved, healthy children, and we lived in suburban satisfaction. We prayed together and never missed a church service, even after I had resigned as pastor from my California parish to accept a generous fellowship offered by a prestigious foundation. We moved to Minnesota where I became a full-time psychology student in pursuit of a bright, new career, while my wife and family rooted for me from the sidelines. I told myself, "God's in His heaven; all's right with the world."

One day I came home from campus and went to the kitchen for a snack. There, to my dismay, I found a book on how to go about getting a divorce. My wife told me—simply, no room for discussion—our marriage was over.

I was thunderstruck. Although we'd had our quarrels and spats, I hadn't suspected the depth of her negative feelings. Apparently, I'd failed to take her complaints seriously enough. But how had it come to this?

From that day on, things moved so quickly. A court order was slapped in my hand, compelling me to leave nearly everything I thought was mine and move out. I was catapulted out of my initial numbness "freeze," and crash-landed at the bottom of my emotions.

The pain was most intense on my final day at home. My heart was like lead. I walked in the door from school that last time after my wife had already left for an evening class at the university. My four little children were tearful but uncomprehending. They'd been told only that I'd be moving out—and that I wouldn't live with them anymore. Like so many in their situation, the kids mistakenly thought they themselves were responsible, when in truth they were being pulled apart by their love for the two adults who could not manage to solve their own problems. Needing to do something to help, they prepared "dinner."

In spite of the welling tears I was fighting, I had to smile at the "special" salad. The little girls had torn up several sticks of their precious bubble gum, mixing it in with lettuce and other greens. In the strange numbness of the moment, I puzzled about whether to really eat the bubble gum bits or save them to chew later.

By the time I walked out the front door, suitcases in hand, I'd learned that it's easier to *eat* bubble gum when your heart is breaking.

Though I fought against the inevitable, you can't successfully contest a divorce. When there was no way to forestall it any longer, the divorce became final.

One of my greatest difficulties was that I'd thought divorce could never happen to me. I'd always believed that if you behave right, try hard and pray, God will see that all goes well, particularly in family relationships. Wasn't it an absolute rule that "the family that prays together stays together"? My own parents had been divorced when I was five, a starting point for many hardships. Like most children of divorced parents, I had resolved to do everything to have a good marriage. So we'd gotten counseling for our disagreements. Why weren't the "rules" working?

I had been confident about our marriage. I knew I could make it good. Success had always come easy.

I had breezed through seminary, held two pastorates, and made it into a clinical psychology program that admitted only about five percent of those who applied! How easy it had been to win a Wheat Ridge fellowship that, quite simply, paid for everything involved in obtaining a Ph.D. from one of the most prestigious programs in the country. Though I was a worrier, I don't think I seriously imagined that anything bad could happen to me. Without putting it in so many words, I was thanking God that I was not as other men are.

And it wasn't only that my marriage and family were decimated. That was painful enough. But somehow *I* had failed completely. I felt like a misfit among other men. They had secure homes and warm families to return to at night; because I was a misfit, I had nobody. It hurt even more to sense that my children shared shame, as children do when they suffer the humiliation of a collapsed home. Well-meaning friends assured me that I was probably better off, or that I would remarry and have another family. But I couldn't imagine it. As I saw it, I had nothing worthwhile to live for.

Emotionally, I careened from one reaction to another, like a silver shot in a pinball machine. I was cynical. I was cool. I blamed whomever I could find to blame. Even the judge—by what right did another man, who had never laid eyes on me, command that I be deprived of the people who meant everything to me and the possessions I had worked so hard for? The anguish in the eyes of my ten-year-old son as he explained to everyone that his parents were getting divorced made me furious. It was wrong that he and his sisters should bear all this grief when they had done nothing to cause it. I wanted to get even with the law, the courts, my wife.

Even psychology offered no help. I'd studied counseling, mastered personality theories, and acquired the best human wisdom about behavior. But it didn't patch up my home, and it didn't patch me up either. My last supporting beam was kicked out from under me.

Before I continue my story, I want to point out something I only saw much later. There were things I had done to contribute to my loss and pain, and things done to me that were beyond my control. Focusing on the *externals* of my dilemma, however, kept me from paying attention to what was going on at a deeper level—the level of the soul. It is from this level, the Bible says, that the issues, or urgent matters of life, are directed (see Prov. 4:23).

Because I did not know how to arm or defend myself

at this spiritual level, confusion set in—and that is the most debilitating darkness of all. God hates divorce; I knew that. I also knew the Bible declared that God is pure love, and that He does no wrong. So how could He allow this evil to crush me and my precious family—without doing a *thing* to stop it? He could have prevented this tragedy. Confusion led to irritation—and to another feeling that frayed at the edges of my conscious thoughts.

Once I abandoned my trust in God, I was steps closer to a spiritual chasm called *despair*. For several reasons, I could not see my true spiritual state at that time.

My theological training at Concordia Seminary, St. Louis, was conservative and grounded in the Scriptures. But the first reason for my inner blindness was this: Like most of my contemporaries, I'd been exposed to the latest, "fashionable" theologians, who taught that the Bible is a flawed book, of human origin, that its claims must be weighed by human judgment. They taught that, although the Bible *contains* God's truth, it is by no means totally true, and I'd hardly noticed that some of these notions had filtered in among my own beliefs.

Second, as a psychology student, I was coming to think of scientific knowledge as nearly infallible. If you couldn't believe the Bible 100 percent of the time, you could rest assured that scientists, basing their findings on "sure and certain" observations, would come up with the truth.

Third—and without realizing what was happening to me—I'd formed something like a subliminal creed: God is an unknowable puzzle; science is man's best hope; and my own "needs" were the best guides as to my choice of lifestyle. What I told myself was that I had suffered deep wounds through no fault of my own (as I thought), and so I should look to something other than an uncaring God for solace. What I did not even imagine was that I had actually replaced the true God—that I had moved some shadowy *other* into His place.

My "solution" to the pain may differ from what you'd

choose. It would be a long while until I understood what false god I'd slipped into the place of the true God because I complicated my already-confused life by turning to alcohol.

Now I began drinking seriously, though I'd rarely used it in excess before. Alcohol became the mainstay of many an evening, alone or with "friends," and I began to experiment with other sins as well. I still went to church every Sunday, still prayed, read the Bible and instructed my children in Christian doctrine when we were together. But some mornings, I couldn't remember what went on the night before. Once, the bumper of my car was grotesquely mangled. What had I done? Where had I been? Had I hurt someone? In my sick insides, fear and shame competed for first place.

Why was I doing this—to hurt myself? No. To hurt God? I never said, "Take that, God," but I truly believed my hurt was His fault. He had betrayed me, let me down, failed to protect me, ignored my record of faithful service *and* broken all promises to hear and answer prayer. He had chosen what was bad for me, and not something good. Underneath it all, I had a big, hot disagreement with God. A major rift. I can remember the anger breaking out into rage one night when I was driving home from a party I have long since forgotten. I don't even recall what trivial frustration had set off the outburst of fury, but I remember well how violently I stormed and shouted at God.

But God is in the business of healing spiritual rifts—rebuilding broken bridges if we will only let Him. For me, the first approach happened this way.

I heard a rumor that a friend had a life-revolutionizing experience with God. That was ridiculous! An experience with God? Something to do with the Holy Spirit? Definitely *weird*. God never did anything palpable in our time, and I decided my friend's experience was some form of self-deception or hysteria.

Yet, I remembered something that gave me pause—

hadn't another friend written to me of a similar experience? He said God had become "real" to him and turned his life and pastoral ministry around. It couldn't hurt to find out a little more.

I began to read books and listen to tapes that made this claim: Anyone who truly calls upon God, no matter what his personal state, can experience His love, His forgiveness and His presence. A dozen conflicting thoughts and emotions rose in me. I was a confirmed Christian: I believed in the Father, Son and Holy Spirit, no question. What were these people talking about? Why should I believe these reports when God had so let me down?

On the other hand, my life was a mess. What did I have to lose? Skeptically, and with many reservations, I began praying something like, "Please give me that experience too. But when and if you do, God, don't make things too difficult."

Nothing happened. *Of course not,* I smirked.

Then a third friend came for a visit. He also claimed he'd experienced "the reality of the living God." He even insisted that God does *miracles* today!

"It's all coincidence, illusion, and the power of suggestion!" I argued.

He reminded me of God's great love for me in sending His Son to die a terrible death on a cross. Though I knew that intellectually, it did no good.

On the last morning of his visit, in the middle of an argument, something happened that was totally different from anything I'd experienced in my forty-five years of life. I was arguing (*for* my own position and *against* "all this scriptural stuff") when I suddenly fell silent in mid-sentence. Quite literally, the speech centers of my brain were actually vacant. No words were there. I moved my lips, but instead the tears began to flow, and in a moment I was sobbing.

Here was the really odd thing: I felt a new kind of sorrow—not pity for myself, but a grieving over what I had done with God! Because I was suffering, I had turned on Him, doubted Him, blamed Him and hardened myself against Him. *I was angry.* There was a rift between us, and I now saw that I had created it. I had been so wrong about Him.

That morning I asked God to forgive me, to cleanse me, and to restore—not my lost family and possessions but my *soul.*

But it was when my friend prayed for me that it occurred.

At first, there was only a waiting silence. Then, He was unmistakably there, just as His Word promises He will be, and I felt His holy presence. For the first time, I really felt His love—directly, perceptibly, in the center of my being. I sensed His nearness and His willingness to heal the rift between us, notwithstanding all I had done to widen it. He came to me in spite of my unbelief, my furious rebellion, even my deliberate decisions to do wrong.

For many days and weeks after, when I opened the Bible to read, the words vibrated with life. More than that, I knew in the core of my being that these words were true no matter what the "scientific" critics said. My heart was changed, and now I wanted to please Him even more than I wanted those things I'd considered precious above all else—and to trust Him no matter what.

Later, too, I discovered my interest in alcohol had disappeared. I have never had a desire to drink alcohol since that day in 1971—over eighteen years ago. This I hesitate to mention because God doesn't always work in the same way. I know many who struggle with dependence on alcohol and tobacco long after they encounter God, and I don't want to give the impression that there is something wrong with others who don't experience the instant deliverance I was given. Nor does He reveal himself only to "special people." He wants to reveal himself to anyone who seeks Him, no matter what their difficulties may be.

I know now that God has laid out a particular path for

each individual, and what He chooses is the best path.

Did I say His choices were *best*? Yes, my self-talk—the things I said in my heart—began to change and to incorporate pure, life-giving truth. As I continually told myself the truth about God, sorrow and depression lifted. I'd heard about joy, and had tried without success to find it in alcohol and sensory stimulation. I now knew where to find it, along with peace and a sense of well-being. My mind was being changed—and so was my life, from the inside out. I'd begun my own journey "home" to the heart of the Father.

Life—From a New Starting Point

Repentance means getting a new mind, according to the literal sense of the New Testament word. As my mind exchanged old lies, or misbeliefs, for the truth about God, His reality, and His care, falsehoods had to yield their grip. You see, an encounter with God in the person of the Holy Spirit does far more important things for you than giving tingles in your solar plexus; it is an encounter with the One whom Jesus called "the Spirit of truth" (John 16:13). He is not just an afterthought in the Trinity. He comes with life-changing power (Philippians 2:13). One way His power is manifested is in dispelling the darkness of doubt, falsehood and unbeliefs with the light of truth. Or, to say it another way, *power lies in the truth.*

Getting truth into my self-talk began immediately, and it's now a process that continues to this day. I've had to face other major crises. And I believe that doubt, questioning, arguing, and seeing no answer are part of life. What I *now* know is that I can rely on the Spirit of truth as He teaches me how to scrutinize my self-talk for signs of a rift with God. I can then isolate those misbeliefs that alienate me from God, and replace them with the truth about who He is and what He wants for me.

An important final note: In time, my life has been made

whole. Much of what I had lost, God restored. Candy came to me through no doing of mine. She, too, had encountered the living reality of the Spirit of truth, and had also been taken by Him out of a dangerous, abusive relationship with alcohol. We were married, and in a few months a judge decided to accede to the requests of my children and let them move into our home.

But the most important changes have occurred *within.*

This morning, for instance, as I listened to the transcendent praise of Bach's incomparable *Gloria in Excelsis* from the Mass in B minor, I felt a spontaneous welling up in thanksgiving and adoration to God. This experience always has an uncanny *newness* whenever it happens. My mind goes back to the time when there was no way I could praise God from my heart.

Then, I said, "Only when God does something about the wreckage in my life will I recognize Him as God again. It all depends on whether He changes my circumstances and gets rid of my misery. If He doesn't, it's because He's powerless or a fraud."

In short, I had it *backward.* I thought my angry rift with God was a result of His failure to act the way He should in my life. But *I* was causing the rift by kicking and struggling against God. Even though my circumstances were painful, ironically, it was my own disagreement with God that brought on an even deeper pain and alienation, the worst I had ever known. The ache that drove me to alcohol was the *result* of the rift I had made; I had thought it was proof that I was justified in my anger. Had I not discovered this reversed view of the truth, I might have sunk to the bottom of my life and drowned there.

My chance to look back at this experience—and to observe the lives of countless clients—only came by His sheer kindness and love. And, as Martin Luther put it, "without any merit or worthiness in me," I have learned that persistent unpleasant emotions can usually be traced back to a rift with God in the soul—one that can remain hidden even from the sufferer for a long time.[1] Unless the misery is due purely and simply to chemical abnormalities (as in some depressions), emotional pain most often generates from faulty beliefs we rehearse in our minds. These misbeliefs amount to a quarrel with God over the path He has chosen for us to walk.

This quarrel can take several forms.

For some their quarrel begins when they believe a lesser good will be the best thing for them. We say things like this: "If only I could get into *this* school"; "I must have *that* job"; "I'll be miserable if he/she won't love me"; "Why can't life be the way *I* want it, right *now*?"

For others, the quarrel comes in believing a bad thing is truly good. We say: "*Why* is it so wrong to sleep with someone you're not married to?"; "Why can't I lie if it will help me or someone else?"; "It shouldn't be considered wrong of me to leave my wife and family—not if I'll be more fulfilled."

And for still others, the problem erupts from believing the reverse—that something good is actually bad. Like Jack, in our opening parable, we say: "*Nobody* tells *me* what to do"; "It's *my* life, and if anyone else is concerned about the choices I make, it's their problem"; "Love? Commitment? *Marriage?* All that does is give somebody a license to run your life."

Always, ultimately, our disputes come back to a quarrel, or rift—not with an impersonal universe, but with *Someone.*

---

[1] I discovered the central importance of this rift by studying the writings of cognitive psychologists like A. T. Beck, Albert Ellis, Russell and Ingrid Grieger, D. Meichenbaum, R. Novaco, Gary Emery, and many others. Even more to the point are the writings of St. Paul (especially his letter to the Romans), the Psalms, and the teachings of Jesus. This discovery has been confirmed in countless clinical conversations. In fact, most emotional problems ultimately result from disagreement with God! To get at this root, we may need to go deeper than we have gone before.

Our biggest problem, then, is not depression, anxiety, or anger. It's not our past history, difficult and ugly as that may be. Nor is it sickness, an accident, loss or affliction. Our greatest problem is not even the sins we commit. It is the deep crevice that wants to open in your soul and mine separating us from the love, joy and peace of a life lived in the closest possible union with our Creator.

This book is written to those who are tired of the pain and the searching and the emptiness—to those who are ready to stop running from one compulsion to another, from counselor to counselor, and who long to stand on the bedrock of life's meaning and purpose.

I know from experience that God's unchanging desire is to come close to you and me, to walk closely with us and, like a father, to wrap us in His love which contains all that we need and takes the place of all that we don't know.

His invitation to you, if life has simply stopped working, is for you to come home to where His heart beats brightly as He hopes for your return. His call, through the prophet Isaiah, is offered to you today: "Come, let's reason together!"

That is the journey we can now begin.

Accusation

You have broken my heart.
O Galilean God-man,
because you did not come
when most I needed you.

You have broken my trust,
O Galilean God-man.
How can I ask for anything, believing,
when so mysteriously and darkly
you turned your back
and did not come to him?

You could have healed him,
Galilean God-man!
You could have,
even at that fateful moment,
torn the gun away
or caused it to misfire,
And yet you hid your face
behind the empty skies.

You have broken my wings,
O Galilean God-man.
I try to lift them up,
to soar to you as in the former days,
but I've become so weak and heavy-hearted
that only through death's gateway
will I fly again.

Martha said to Jesus,
"Lord, if you had been here,
my brother would not have died."
Jesus said to her,
"Your brother will rise again."

For a brief moment I forsook you,
but with great compassion I will gather you.
In overflowing wrath for a moment
I hid my face from you,
but with everlasting love
I will have compassion on you,
says the Lord, your Redeemer.

TWO

When the Pain Won't Quit

Ernest Hemingway once said, "Life breaks us all, and afterward many are strong at the broken places." I would say *some* are strong at the broken places. Most stay broken and hurting at those broken places. Why? Because so many hide their wounds, *trying* to be strong, trying to be "adult," and even denying there was a break in the first place. Others spend their time looking for a "quick-fix" answer, compulsively looking for someone, anyone, who can tell them how to master and change their external circumstances or relationships, when the problem is a rift at the bottom of their own souls.

When I was in my own private pit of despair I was of the latter sort. I tried everything. Marriage counseling. Psychotherapy. Religion. Nothing had worked to solve my problem or touch my pain. In my counseling practice, I've heard these words—"I've tried everything"—many times from those who have never quite recovered from the sudden loss of a loved one, or from the disclosure of a spouse's illicit affair, or a rudely shut door of opportunity, or disappointing rejection, or frustrated ambition, or even from turning forty.

Many of these folks have tried to anesthetize themselves with alcohol, while others "soften the blow" with drugs. Others get "into" pseudo-spiritual movements, reciting *whistle-in-the-dark, every-cloud-has-a-silver-lining, it'll-all-come-out-in-the-wash-so-cheer-up* phrases, only to discover that they're hollow. Some try pouring on Christian practices: "I'll go to church more, pray longer, give more." Psychologists have described a type who try to erase their troubles by plunging into affairs, trafficking with sex vendors, indulging their perversions to the max, inundating their senses. The less sensuous soak themselves in work to produce transitory amnesia. Lately, visualization has gotten big play, as have audio tapes with so-called "subliminal" inspirational messages hidden under music. Many practice Yoga, transcendental meditation, psychic mind control and chatting with "ascended masters," carrying on affairs with strange gods.

Most have not overlooked counseling. They go to their pastors asking for help, and many pastors give themselves generously (sometimes more generously than they can afford) to the cure of individual souls. This ministry succeeds in building faith and resolving the difficulties of many. But too often, pastors are left with frustration when the one they are counseling will not or cannot be helped. Psychologists and psychiatrists, too, encounter individuals they are unable to help, and many of them cannot conceive that the true field of conflict lies deeper than the unconscious mind.

So, even after wearing out several pastors and counselors, the desperate, hurting soul sometimes says, "I've tried everything. *Nothing* helps."

When nothing works—and nothing else is a true, permanent solution—I maintain that it's time to go deeper.

Let me tell you about Marta, a woman who thought *she* had tried everything before she learned the *real* first mile on the journey back to health and happiness.

Marta

The silence that hung between us in my consulting room gave me a few moments to observe. The sad woman sitting across from me had stopped talking and was staring vacantly out the window at the tops of the trees. She was slightly overweight, an unkempt and no longer young blond who might once have been good-looking.

Really, I thought, *she's no different from others I've known at church, or friends I've met outside the clinic—even members of my family.* Many times, I'd been impressed that my clients are not a group of strange beings from some other planet, even though some still think that way about people who consult psychologists. My clients are just ordinary people who have turned to a psychologist for help with problems common to the human race.

I had learned that Marta's depression had begun some four years before. Backing her car out of the garage one day, she did not see that her toddler had wandered into the driveway. She'd run over her own child, crushing the little one's chest.

After the funeral—a terrible ordeal—Marta blamed herself unmercifully. Guilt and self-reproach dug into her heart. Very soon, Marta came to despise her own reflection in the mirror. She had stopped enjoying life and everything in it and even punished herself by letting her appearance go. No one could convince her that she had any personal worth, for she saw herself as the bloodied killer of her own child.

Those who sought to help Marta had told her she was wrong in blaming herself, that she was obviously innocent: it was an accident. The words did not penetrate. After counseling with her pastor, a psychotherapist struck some pay dirt when he learned of her relationship with her fault-finding parents. He said the problem was that Marta was determined to blame herself. He put her on antidepressant medication for eighteen months. Even that didn't help.

When she came to me, she believed I was her last resource. It was a grim situation. "I forgot to tell you," Marta said, abruptly coming out of her own thoughts. "I even stopped eating sugar because a friend thought I had the 'sugar blues.' Then I tried aerobic exercises, massage and acupuncture. Some friends in my church said I had evil spirits, so I had prayer ministry to cast them out. Something did seem to lift a little, but it didn't make me feel any better in the long run. Finally, my friends got tired of listening to me. They told me my whole problem is that I'm just full of self-pity. They're fed up—and I am, too!"

As we continued to meet, I noticed something in Marta, which she betrayed more by hints than by telling me directly. For instance, when I asked her what happened when she prayed, she replied that her mind was empty. Then she muttered, "It seems to me it's God's turn to talk, anyway." Another time she mentioned that people who think prayer will change things are naive. And there was a casual remark about the literature in our waiting room: "Too fundamentalist." Most of the time, though, Marta was on her guard, so these wisps of feelings slipped out only rarely.

What I observed, despite Marta's control, was that she was deeply, deeply angry, and not just on occasion but all the time. I also realized that she had no awareness of it. Something, at a deep level, was very wrong, and Marta was fighting to keep it out of the spotlight of her own awareness.

The closest she came was the morning she began her session with these words: "You know, I think I have a bone to pick with the Lord. I think I'm upset because He . . . because God allowed me to . . . you know . . ." Her voice trailed off. Then she covered it all up again, saying, "Well, maybe I'm just having a bad day!"

So for some time, the deeper issue remained hidden; buried.

Observations

Let's step away from Marta's story briefly to pose some urgent questions.

Why is it that Marta and many like her continue to ignore or hide the real issue? Why do people deny that anger at God may be the real root of their illness?

One possibility is that they just don't see it. But there's another reason as well: Most people think that anger at God is too hot to handle. At some level they may know they have a quarrel, a separation, a falling out with God, but they cover it up because it's too terrible to admit.

Why is it too terrible? Because of fear. *What would* God do if He knew. . . ? What would that say about me as a person? As a Christian?

What our anger at God *really* reveals is that at the base of our beliefs (what we consciously *say* we believe) lies another level of thought (what we *really* believe). And when what we really believe separates us from God, then we are suffering from *misbeliefs*.

Since I have used the term *misbeliefs* several times already, I want to demonstrate what it means by way of some examples:

"After God has done so much for me—sending His Son to die on the cross and all—I'd be ungrateful if I admitted to a conflict with Him."

"God wouldn't understand my problem with Him, and He'd only tell me to 'shape up.' "

"I can't let myself feel anger at Him; He's so big He could wipe me out."

"If I let out any upset feelings toward Him, He might get really angry and take away the few blessings I have. He might want to show me how bad it can get!"

"If I admitted that I'm quarreling with God, it would destroy what's left of my self-image. People think of me as a good Christian. If I were to admit I'm angry at God I'd know I was a total flop."

"I've worked so hard and so long to prove to myself I deserve God's blessings; it would be a failure to find such a flaw in myself."

"Good Christians don't get angry. And they don't ever, ever, ever get into an argument with God!"

"I'd be utterly lost and in total despair if I thought there was anything wrong between God and me."

Why do I call these *misbeliefs*? Because they are beliefs based on misunderstanding, error, or faulty teaching, *not* on the truth of Scripture. (More on this in chapter seven.)

For now, it's enough to know that our misbeliefs cause us to hide from God because we are afraid we will wound, offend, or drive Him away, or because we are terrified that He is out to test our spiritual strength by crushing us. Mostly, these misbeliefs go unnoticed until a crisis comes along. And even in a crisis, when the feelings of anger at God begin to boil, we cover them with self-accusation. The result can be emotional and even physical illness that will not yield to reason or treatment because we think we need to conceal the real root problem: We are accusing God, and who are we to do so?

If right now you're angry with God, you are not the first of His saints to feel such a frightening emotion. If you're in a disagreement with Him and you've been hiding it from yourself, you can only gain by facing reality.

Jonah was angry at God—and the result? God stayed at his side and tried to teach him gentle lessons about his arrogant, judgmental, unforgiving attitude. Job vented his pain and frustration over losing all he held dear, but the Lord's first response was *not* to squash him but to say, "Who is this who darkens my counsel with words without knowledge?" (Job 38:2). Throughout the Scriptures God is revealed as a loving Father, slow to anger, quick to forgive, and One who aches when we hurt (see Exodus 34:6; Deuteronomy 28:1–14; Psalm 30:1–5; Matthew 23:37; Romans 8:31-39).

Most often, in order to get at the anger, there is another, more basic step you must take. It is discovering the misbelief that's feeding your denial.

When She Came to Herself . . .

Marta eventually took the plunge.

I finally approached the "terrifying ground" by asking her if she had ever considered this: that God could have protected her baby if He had chosen to do so, since He is all-powerful and nothing is too hard for Him.

She was shocked that I should even raise the question. "God wanted my baby in heaven. That's the way I like to think about it," she responded. "Everything happens for the best, doesn't it?" The tears began to flow.

"You *like* to think about God taking your baby away from you into heaven?" I prodded. I knew it hurt, but I also sensed that something was about to surface.

More tears. "Yes."

"If you like it so much, why the tears?"

"I—I don't know. It hurts. It's my fault. I hate myself. God seems far away. I don't know . . ."

"You feel so bad about yourself and the baby and God that it makes you weep—even though you tell yourself it's all for the best?"

"Yes, I tell myself that. But it seems phony. I want my baby."

"In spite of your best efforts, the pain hasn't let up, and you don't know why."

"If I had only been paying attention to what I was doing that day. I don't know why any of this happened in the first place. Why *my* baby? Why couldn't God have stopped me? Warned me. Done *something*?"

"Although you see the whole thing as your fault," I pursued, "you still wonder about God. You wonder why God wanted to take *your* child? What made Him do such a thing to *you*?"

"I don't want to blame God; it's not His fault. It's *mine*. But . . . I'm so confused."

"You have no intention of blaming God, but you can't help thinking that He could have prevented the accident?

That He could have saved your child. . . ?"

"He's all-powerful. He can do anything. Why didn't He keep it from happening? I can't tell God what He should have done. And I feel so guilty for thinking God is at fault. We're not supposed to have those thoughts, are we?"

"So, you feel terrible about having ideas like these. I suppose you're having some feelings, too, aren't you—feelings that maybe you'd rather not bring out?"

"Other feelings? It's hard to be sure. I think I might be sort of holding it against Him. Isn't that awful? Do you think I'm angry at God? That's really bad, isn't it?"

From that day our ongoing dialogue drew her closer and closer to recovery because we were able to deal with the real, underlying sources of pain. Marta's suffering could not heal because she had hidden, covered over, denied and buried her deep rift with the One who holds the power of life itself. She was covering over her anger at God because it was "too terrible" for her to acknowledge. So she had turned the accusations on herself.

Here is where her misbeliefs came into play—misbeliefs about herself and God. The most obvious misbeliefs were those Marta held about herself. I say obvious because her neglected appearance and the depression suggested to me she was punishing herself for being such a "bad mother" that she had caused her child's death. And it was obvious she had not benefited much from the comfort of the Holy Spirit promised to us in the Bible (see John 14:15–21). On this layer of self-blame but just at the edge of consciousness were other misbeliefs that she barely allowed into her mind because they seemed too hot to hold: "How can I dare to blame God, who is supposed to be all good? How can I dare to be angry at Him since He's all-powerful. Good people never get angry at God; they *only* trust Him, *all* the time. If I'm angry at Him, I must be a terrible person. And terrible persons go to hell."

Beneath all this was a layer of misbeliefs so seared over

by white-hot anger, she had turned her face from them altogether: "God didn't care enough about me or my child to act and save her life. He is heartless and cruel—or He's impotent and a fraud."

Marta knew what she was *supposed* to believe—that God is all-loving and all-powerful. But she could not, or thought she could not, make her head connect with what was in the depths of her heart. With such an awesome gulf opening up within her own soul, it was no wonder she lived in such strong denial. Who could live or function otherwise?

When God Seems Far Off

Those who have experienced the kind of tragic loss and crushing pain Marta did may most readily understand her reasons for denying the anger: It can sometimes feel like a large, furious beast that wants to break through your skin and begin destroying—just destroying. There may also be the sense of trying to "punish" God with angry silence, the way we try to punish another human being who has hurt or angered us, by turning our backs on him.

But other traumas, too—things less dramatic but just as painful as Marta's tragedy—can lead to a lifestyle of denial. I am thinking now of men and women I've known who have suffered such things as:

- neglect, rejection, or abuse by a parent or spouse
- rejection by their own child, or a child's rebellion
- molestation
- a debilitating injury or sickness
- a major financial loss
- emotional or psychological illness

Then there is a different sort of person—those whose denial fits hand-in-glove with an insistence that they be free to do whatever they want, regardless of God's order, laws and clear guidelines. To them, God had the "audacity" to build His laws into the universe and into human relationships; therefore their struggles and pain are *His* fault, not their own. This is the rift with God felt by the heavy smoker who now has cancer, the homosexual or drug-user who now has AIDS, the guy who had double-martinis for lunch and dinner every day for twenty years and whose liver is now shot, the promiscuous teenager who has gonorrhea. "If God is so kind and loving and pow-erful," they ask bitterly, "why can't He do something to help *me*?" And not these folks only, but others who ignore God's warnings and laws—His *pleas* that we live accord-ing to His guidance. Here are a few of their common com-plaints:

> "Why should it be wrong to leave my husband and children if I'm in love with someone else?"
>
> "My wife has left me. My family fell apart. And I gave them everything they asked for—even if it meant working overtime and being away from home."
>
> "I can't get my husband to change."
>
> "Why don't I stop having 'live-ins' and just get *married*? I don't believe a man should be tied down to just one woman, that's why. I keep telling you, my problem is women. They're so selfish."

Emotional distress, too, can be traced to denial. The sufferer cannot believe that God has his or her best inter-ests in mind—even though they can quote a dozen scrip-tures and sing choruses every Sunday about His unfailing love. I include in this category: worry, fear and mild depres-sion. Again and again I hear:

> "Things never turn out the way I plan. And I've worked so hard to get where I am. I *need* this pro-motion. But I'm terrified I won't get it."
>
> "Of course I worry! Because I know—don't ask me how, I just *know*—that something bad is going to happen to one of my children."

"*Praise?* That's a pretty absurd thing to suggest, considering I'm so depressed. I can't believe you'd suggest something so trite."

"Why am I exhausted? I used to think God answered prayers. But I'm not sitting around waiting for things anymore. I'm a mover-and-shaker. I'm the type who *makes* things happen."

How on earth can I relate all these complaints and symptoms to *denial?* There is only one real root of misbelief at the very bottom of it all. Pulling it up for an examination, it looks like this:

"I know what the Bible says about God, but I just don't believe that He is as good as He claims to be. He must be at fault, because my own feelings, perceptions and beliefs about life cannot be incorrect. I must be right, and He must be wrong."

But who wants to face up to such an audacious and prideful claim? Who would say out loud, "I know better than God. I'm more loving than He is, and I would never have allowed such a thing, made such a law"?

I believe that we *hide* such statements from our own conscious mind all the time. But at the level of our soul, something wants to malign, discredit and defy God. Some would be quick to say it's Satan or a demonic influence (which I won't dispute). But even if the source is outside, it cannot wreak its spiritual havoc in us *unless we agree with its false premises about God.* The flat truth is that there is a force of human pride in each of us that will fight to the death, insisting that we are right and God is wrong. Most times, though, we simply don't want to face the fact that our enemy is *us.* The reason for this blindness, of course, is our sinful, fallen condition. Even after we become Christians our eyes only open to the truth slowly. That's why even good Christians like Marta can bury their rift with God so deep. To say that we don't understand, or that we are hurt and angry, or that we want an accounting from God, means we are not as good and mature as we are "supposed" to be. Better to hide from ourselves. "Better," the self-preserving, sinful nature says, "to think that God is wrong than to admit that I am."

So, from observing the painful struggles of so many, like Marta, I have concluded that there is one starting place for the man or woman who wants to become whole and free again no matter what their inner struggle. That is, to stop denying that they are in a disagreement with God; to face the fact that they may in fact be downright angry with Him. This makes possible the kind of confession that the apostle John described when he wrote:

> If we claim to have fellowship with [God] yet walk in darkness, we lie and do not live by the truth. . . . If we claim to be without sin, we deceive ourselves and the truth is not in us. If we confess our sins, he is faithful and just and will forgive us our sins and purify us from all unrighteousness. (1 John 1:6, 8, 9)

Once we make this kind of confession, it makes possible the next step: God is able to show us how we drifted away from Him in the first place. It is necessary for God to give us this kind of light—to take us to the point inside where our misbeliefs first cut us loose from solid, life-giving dependence upon God, so that we can anchor ourselves firmly in Him.

It's to this second phase of healing that we must now turn.

Wedding Anniversary

I waken early
   on our wedding anniversary,
      beside an empty pillow,
Longing for strong arms to hold me close.
Longing to know
   that I have had a nightmare.

Better to get up and run
   on this oppressive morning.
And so I run, and ache, and weep
   down by the river.
      Alone.
And cry out to the empty sky,
   "Where are you, God,
      Where are you?"
But all I hear
   is distant thunder.

Upon my bed by night
I sought him whom my soul loves;
I sought him, but found him not;
I called him, but he gave no answer.

My God, my God, why have you forsaken me?

                    September 7, 1989.

THREE

Spiritual Drift

How can a *Christian,* one who has been called to dwell in the Father's house, come to feel that he's a great distance from home? How do you and I come to the point where we have a rift with God? Most often, it's because we've forgotten or never knew truths that would anchor us near the safe shores. In short, we simply drift.

Jiff couldn't see the cabin. He rubbed his eyes and brushed his hair out of the way. Was he still asleep? Was this a dream? He shivered. It must have turned colder since he'd stretched out in the boat moored to the family's dock. Boarding the boats alone was forbidden for the eight-year-old, but . . . well . . . the truth was, this scrawny boy loved to gaze at the sky and dream, and had often hidden away in the flat bottom of the aluminum rowboat where, as he thought, he could stay concealed and secure, whatever the grown-ups said.

Blinking, he peered over his shoulder. Wherever he looked he saw nothing but water. Even the riverbanks had faded from view. How had it happened? Where was he?

While his boat had rocked the boy gently to sleep, it had slipped from its moorings and, carried by the current, drifted far down the river. Slowly, Jiff realized that, ever so softly and without his even having an inkling of it, he had drifted to the river's mouth. Now he was in a tiny skiff on the ocean. He couldn't imagine how many miles of water separated him from the comfort of his father's embrace. Nor did he see any way to get back!

"Hey, young fella, whatcha doin' out here?"

Jiff looked behind him and saw a fisherman a hundred feet away.

"I don't know where home is and I don't know how to get there," replied the boy, starting to cry.

"Hang on, sonny, just a minute." The fisherman started his motor and quickly came alongside. "Now tell me how you got out here," he said.

"I fell asleep in my boat up the river and I woke up here."

"Would you like a ride? I'll just tie you up and tow you home. Have to be careful to keep the rope out of the propeller. Can you do that?"

"Sure," returned Jiff, relief in his voice. "But, sir, do you know where I live?"

"No," said the man, "but I'm sure you can recognize it when we get there, can't you?"

"Oh yes. I know exactly how my cabin looks from the river. My dad and I have to know how to get home when we go fishing."

Half an hour later, Jiff was in the arms of his dad. There was no space between them at all!

Like Jiff, we can drift away slowly, imperceptibly. Those who never had a true, personal relationship with God the Father through Jesus Christ can usually understand what this means. Maybe they went to church as children, but got caught up in other interests as time went by. Maybe they even go to church now, but feel it's pretty much a ritual—something they do to keep God "satisfied," or a sedative for inner distress that won't go away, or it's just another step on a vague, spiritual journey. Though these folks, too, may initially feel that God is the One who remains aloof to their pain, they may be more honest about misbeliefs and anger than some who are "born-again, Spirit-filled" Christians.

That is because "born-again" Christians are "supposed" to have all the answers—or at least ready access to them in the Bible. And though we may *know* the Bible backward and forward, most of us have been taught little or nothing about how to draw life from the truth of God's Word that is supposed to be bread to our souls. So, believing with our heads, we drift in our hearts. And when troubles come and God seems distant, we suspect that *He* is to blame.

Not Knowing Your Anchor Is Loosed

I sometimes wonder what my reaction would have been if, back in the lonely, troubled days after my marriage ended, someone had told me that my real problem was not the losses I had sustained but the rift I had created between myself and God. I probably would have disagreed, pointing out that my problems were due to circumstances, other people's actions, and injustice in the system. If there was a rift—*if* there was, and I certainly didn't think there was—then the space between us had been caused by God, for He had failed to support me, and had, in effect, deprived me of what was truly good.

But there was no rift, I would have assured you, based on *my* behavior; no rift that *I* could do anything to change. Wasn't I going regularly to church, praying, even teaching and preaching? Well, maybe not with as much enthusiasm as before, but what could God expect?

I have observed that Christians who are struggling often know *something* is deeply wrong, something more than friends and counselors have suggested—though they themselves hardly know what it is. The notion that it might be a rift between themselves and God, however, is usually too shocking to consider.

A pious visitor once asked Thoreau, "Henry, have you made your peace with God?"

"We have never quarreled," answered the great naturalist sanctimoniously.

Some readers would offer a resounding "Second!" to that.

For example, there was Patrick. He was a tired-looking, graying, middle-aged man, who didn't understand why he was unable to get over a separation from his family, though it had occurred five years before. When I suggested that his real turmoil might be the result of a gap between himself and God, he didn't mince words with me.

"What are you talking about?" he nearly exploded. "I don't have any troubles with God. I've been born again! Baptized. God's Spirit is in me. Your suggestion is ridiculous."

I figured it wouldn't help to argue with Patrick, a stocky, ruddy-complected Chicago Irishman. So I listened, and invited him to take the initiative in our dialogue. As I anticipated, he knew all the right scriptures.

"Doesn't Romans 5:1 say that we have been justified through faith, and we have *peace* with God?" he asked rhetorically, unwilling to entertain the notion he had worked so hard to ignore—that his pain was due to a rift with God, and not to the wrongs done to him by others.

"Could you consider the possibility," I proposed, "that you and I are both right?"

"How do you mean?"

I agreed with him, of course, that God's promises stand firm and once He reclaims us as His children because of Jesus nothing whatever can separate us from Him and His love (see Romans 8:33-39).

But, I reminded him, as long as we trudge around on this planet we carry a burden—the old, sinful nature, sometimes called *the flesh*. This is not the *material* part of us; rather, it's the rebellious, God-despising nature within that existed before we came to Christ (see Romans 8:5—8).

The fact that Scripture tells us to "reckon" ourselves dead to this old nature (Romans 6:11) indicates that it hasn't stopped making trouble. It's permanently allied with Satan, and it advances the devil's program by repeating his lies, much as we defined in the previous chapter.

"The rift begins," I explained to Patrick, "when we *suspect* Him of not being good to us. From there, we gradually talk ourselves out of the security His presence gives. Faith is the Bible's word for our side of the relationship with God. It describes the part we play. And the rift comes when we distort or weaken our faith.

"When we buy the lies of the devil and the old nature, they become *our* misbeliefs. And we repeat these wrong ideas over and over to ourselves, never noticing that they're false."

When that happens, I told him, we become "double-minded"—something the apostle James warned against (see James 1:5–8). That is, our faith gets mixed with false beliefs, and the result is anti-faith, which pushes us away from our heavenly Father. Someone has put it this way: We become "partial believers."

"So you see, the wedge is driven from our side, not from God's," I concluded.

Patrick was able to recognize his struggle with double-mindedness, and it helped him begin the healing process.

Misbeliefs: The "Anti-faith" of the Old Nature

Here are some of the misbeliefs pushed on us by the old sinful nature. When you rehearse these in your self-talk, you are drifting, widening your rift with God:

"God can't be who He says He is, or He wouldn't treat me so badly."

"I know the Bible says all this wonderful stuff about God, but I'm certainly not experiencing it. So maybe it's not true."

"People tell me what God has done for *them*, and that's fine. But I guess He doesn't care enough to help me!"

"I used to think He was blessing me and answering my prayers—but as I think about it, all those things could have been coincidental."

"Who am I to think God would pay any attention to me? I'm so insignificant and unimportant! Nobody else cares. Why should He?"

When we let the unbelief of our old sinful nature mix into our minds, scrambling up what we know is true about our heavenly Father, we are open for trouble. We sense God's presence less, and imagine that He's stepped away. Soon we lose sight of Him and begin to do our own thing. So we let ourselves become *mis*believers when God wants to help us to fix upon the truth, which keeps us close to Him!

When God's "Strong" Ones Slide

Even God's most exemplary children—strong believers—have times when they feel estranged from God and tell themselves it's His fault.

David, for example, cried, "Why, O Lord, do you stand far off? Why do you hide yourself in times of trouble?" (Psalm 10:1). And he pleaded, "Awake, O Lord! Why do you sleep? Rouse yourself! Do not reject us forever. Why do you hide your face and forget our misery and oppression?" (Psalm 44:23, 24).

Through the prophets, God gave us His perspective on the true state of things: "Your iniquities have separated you from your God, and your sins have hidden his face from you, so that he will not hear" (Isaiah 59:2). In short, Isaiah was saying, "God doesn't hide, or stand afar off, or sleep, or forget us. The separation is of our own making."

The Galatians were also putting distance between themselves and God, and Paul warned them: "But now that you know God—or rather are known by God—how is it that you are turning back to those weak and miserable principles?" (Galatians 4:9). And, writing to his Corinthian converts, Paul wrote them to receive healing for their rift! "We are . . . Christ's ambassadors, as though God were making his appeal through us. We implore you on Christ's behalf: *Be reconciled to God*" (2 Corinthians 5:20, italics mine).

These New Testament converts, like us, tasted the sweetness of Christ but they were at odds with the Lord because of their own misbeliefs. Ironically, the Galatians could not believe what God had told them about His love, and the Corinthians could not believe what He'd told them about His holiness. Both groups were sliding into error, because they had turned away from the truth and re-aligned their beliefs with the devil's propaganda. And the result was that they told themselves in some way that God and His message to them were wrong!

When our pure faith becomes mixed with error and falsehood, we have taken hold of the greatest lie in the universe: *God is wrong.* This lie is the great axe that severs the root of faith.

When I saw a bomb fall on my marriage and family, I attributed the tragedy to my wife's immaturity, to the in-ordinate demands of my professional and academic tasks, to the worldly ideology in which we had been immersed as students at a secular university, and to an endless array of maladjustments and system-defects. I even went to a psychotherapist and learned that I had often communi-cated poorly. True enough, I admit sadly. But deep inside, *I blamed God because He could have stopped the out-working of evil had He chosen to.*

Does God do wrong? Of course not. Do we accuse Him of wrongdoing? Most of us, like Marta in Chapter Two, would never dream of accusing Him in so many words. But when we disagree with Him, we are saying *indirectly* that He is in the wrong.

For example, just the other day a young woman con-fided: "I was an enthusiastic Christian, really gung-ho. Then my father had a stroke. God let him suffer. Just look-ing at him took away my peace with God. Now I don't know—I go to church, but that's about all. Dad's suffering really ruined my faith."

E. Stanley Jones wrote that at his daughter's graduation another graduate turned to wave goodbye to her friends on the hills above. She stepped back to lean against a low wall—or so she thought. There was nothing but a sheer drop. Down she fell, two hundred feet, to her death. She was a widowed mother's only daughter.

When such senseless tragedies occur without God making a move to stop them, don't many of us tuck angry little thoughts about God in a secret pocket in our hearts, where we think He won't see them?

Sometimes even "strong" Christians suddenly break off their relationship with God altogether. They quit. They decide that God isn't accessible, or that God doesn't exist. Some are like the seminary professor, also described by E. Stanley Jones, who had been struck by a truck and suffered a broken leg. After a long and tiresome convalescence, at his first appearance in chapel services, he said to the students: "I no longer believe in a personal God. If there were a personal God, he surely would have whispered to me to beware of the danger of the oncoming truck and saved me from this calamity!" For him, and for many others, the way to handle anger is to erase God as a person. The truth is, this is only the final stroke in a separation that begins with small, threadlike cracks of misbelief.

Perhaps you, too, have felt—without daring to utter it in words—that God somehow let you down. Perhaps you haven't carried your misbeliefs to the point of unbelief, like the professor who denied God's existence; but even the strongest of us wonder at senseless suffering.

One of the greatest illustrations of our struggle between faith and unbelief was written by the Russian Christian novelist Dostoyevsky. In his book *The Brothers Karamazov*, he tells of Ivan—a sensitive, caring intellectual to whom innocent suffering is morally unacceptable. Ivan shocks and unsettles his listeners by telling of a five-year-old girl who was subjected to every possible torture by her educated parents. She had nowhere to go, no one to run to for protection. Her parents beat her, birched her, kicked her till her body was covered with bruises. They then shut her up all night, in the cold and frost, in the outdoor privy. For wetting her bed they smeared her face with excrement and made her eat it.

"Do you realize," Ivan cries, "what it means when a little creature like that, who's quite unable to understand what's happening to her, beats her little aching chest in that vile place, in the dark and cold, with her tiny fist and weeps searing, unresentful and gentle tears to 'dear kind God' to protect her? Can you understand all this absurd and horrible business. . . ? Why, the whole world of knowledge [of good and evil] isn't worth that child's tears to her 'dear kind God'!" Ivan concludes that because of such unheeded suffering, he must be an atheist.

As you read the description of the little girl's suffering, you may actually feel Ivan's shock and anger, for Dostoyevsky was a skillful writer. But it is more likely that you've already experienced similar emotions yourself when you've had to confront innocent suffering, whether your own or someone else's, and it was Dostoyevsky's intention to touch and awaken those feelings.

Maybe you haven't rejected God, but surely you've sensed the soul-rending tension between God's goodness, power and promises on the one hand and unanswered prayers or shocking, senseless loss on the other. And in such tension, you may have asked yourself if, maybe, in some way, God could be wrong. Unless we find God's remedy for this rift that lies at the bottom of our souls, we gradually drift, becoming doubters, critics, cynics. Or else we'll live as troubled believers, trying our best not to give in to frightening notions.

Everything, as Dostoyevsky would say, depends on faith and what we do with it.

A Spiritual Disease

When we sense something deeply unsettled about our souls, we may seek psychological help, or counseling from a pastor—or we may not. We may conceive of our problems vaguely or precisely. We may describe ourselves as depressed, distraught, nervous, agitated, bound up, easily upset, irritable, insomniac, losing or gaining weight, unhappy, or losing interest in life. We may decide to stifle our troubles with God by plunging into deliberate sin. We may even manifest physical problems: stomach trouble, headaches, muscle tension, digestive difficulties, and tremors, among other complaints.

If, in addition, we feel "far from God" or appear to have lost most of our interest in God, the Word and prayer, muttering about how little good Christianity has done for us, we may have a problem that is primarily spiritual—an aching, aggravated separation from God.

Let's examine, more carefully and specifically, both the symptoms and the roots of infirmities that come from this rift.

Bittersweet

Remember
when you brought me
    Bittersweet
a hundred years ago,
    or yesterday?
Bright berries, tucked among
    the trophies of the hunt.
Today, my love, I gather
    Bittersweet,
    bright orange
against a grey November sky,
    and I remember
        You.

Behold, I have engraved you
on the palms of my hands.

Call me no more Naomi, but call me Mara,
For the Lord has dealt bitterly with me.

Remember my affliction and my bitterness!
My soul continually thinks of it
and is bowed down within me.
But this I call to mind,
and therefore I have hope:
The steadfast love of the Lord never ceases,
His mercies never come to an end;
They are new every morning;
Great is thy faithfulness.
"The Lord is my portion," says my soul,
"Therefore I will hope in him."

FOUR

The Big Distractions

As we've seen in the previous chapter, even men and women who are trying to walk in the truth can wind up far from God. We drift because the anchoring truths of God's love for us are not in place; because those "anchors" slip from the sandy sub-floor of a wounded soul; because it is fearful to admit we're angry at God and so we cover our sense of distance from Him with denial. Any one of these factors, or all of them in combination, will put the soul to sleep, so that when and if you wake up to the pain, you find yourself at a great distance from God—and angry that "He moved."

I know a Christian counselor whose stock in trade is emotional honesty, and who buys every book he can find on how to make this inner honesty work in one's life so that the person will remain healthy and free. He knows when others need to tell themselves the truth—but he seems to have missed the fact that his spirit is clouded with misbeliefs that cause him painful consequences. He is like the physician who carefully tends others, while treating a gashed artery in his own body with Band-Aids.

Does that sound peculiar? All too often intelligent, spiritually sensitive men and women *keep* themselves oblivious to the truth behind their own difficulties. How often have you heard about a man or woman who sensed something was wrong in their marriage but decided to ignore the signals because they wanted to think the problem would pass? Or how about the person who finds a painful lump but refuses to go to the doctor because it might be cancer? Does this make sense? No. But it happens all the time.

Denial, as we've seen, is one reason we drift away from God. But, assuming we get past the denial stage, it's all too easy to focus on the symptoms of our problem rather than the problem itself. Our symptoms may include: depression, anxiety, fear, anger (in all their attendant emotional, spiritual and physiological manifestations), a sense of meaninglessness, reliance on alcohol and drugs, ingratitude, self-centeredness, cynicism, and even legalism and fake religiosity. This, of course, is not a complete list, but covers the most common symptoms with which Christians struggle, and which can be distractions from the real, underlying spiritual "disease."

Let's examine each symptom to see how it may be founded on a misbelief that leads to a rift with God. Each symptom is not *invariably* caused by the rift, but, taken together with other signs, may denote that you and I are suffering from what I refer to as a *rift syndrome.* We will not discuss at this time *how* to begin the healing process; it is important now that you see the clear disparity between God's offer of life and health and the various states in which the rift syndrome can leave you.

A Closer Look

Depression . . . Apathy . . . Unhappiness. Perhaps you've heard yourself say internally: "I feel as if nothing is worth doing," or "My life is not worthwhile," or "I am a loser, a failure," or "There's no point in getting out of bed." Emotional distress or "flatness" may, of course, signify biochemical disturbances, or even such things as the effects of changing seasons and variations in light. You cannot conclude that the problem is a rift with God solely on the basis of feeling bad. But persistent negative feelings are, nevertheless, the most easily noticed symptom of the rift. To live in such a depressed state flies in the face of the Bible's teaching that God is the Father of lights; the giver of good and perfect gifts, including a purposeful life (see Psalm 139; James 1:17, 18).

Anxiety . . . Fearfulness . . ."Stress." Do you frequently experience fear, over-alertness, nervous tension, difficulty relaxing or resting, concentration problems? Or physiological symptoms like a rapid heartbeat, palpitations, excessive sweating, dry mouth, trembling, tightness in the muscles? These are symptoms of *anxiety and fear*, and may also warn of a rift with God.

I once had some conversations with a twenty-year-old athlete I'll call Tyler. This well-built college sophomore shook throughout our first meeting as if he were having delirium tremens. But his reaction had nothing to do with a hangover.

As we talked, I learned that Tyler's life was haunted by dread, controlled by some inner "prophecy" that sooner or later his strength would fail him. "I feel like there's a judgment hanging over my head," he told me. "I know I'll be on a date, and some bigger and stronger guy will go after my girl. I won't be able to defend her, and he'll punch me around. She'll think I'm not man enough, and she'll go off with the guy. I'll be left. I feel like such a puny wimp."

Regaling himself constantly with that kind of self-talk, it's no wonder Tyler had a tremor.

Tyler's self-talk did not so much reveal a dislike for himself as a disconnection from the Source of all power. In this case, our talks uncovered a major rift with God fairly quickly.

During early adolescence he'd been close to God, but later he turned aside from his Christian walk in pursuit of what he considered a more pleasurable agenda. As a result, he had no reason to trust the God he had turned away from, and no sense that God would protect him. Instead, he feared that God would expose as a false god the idol Tyler had made of his own masculinity. (More on this aspect later.) So every day was like walking out on thinning ice, with dark waters waiting beneath the spidering cracks. It was no wonder he literally trembled.

I wish I could tell you Tyler was healed. He improved some, but sidestepped my best efforts to persuade him to look at his rift with God. He barely admitted to fears about his masculinity (what secular psychologists would consider his root problem), let alone his disagreement with God. *His* god (that is, the unbridled pleasures of mascu-. linity) couldn't be wrong. So he just did away with the true God, using the usual, flippant response that the Bible was written by old-fashioned legalists. Never mind that his foray into free sex was causing him incredible anxiety.

These symptoms of fear and anxiety can mean you are running from God, the very One who promises protection (see Psalm 18:23, 42) and rest for anxious, weary souls (see Matthew 11:28). I believe this was the case with Tyler.

Anger. This includes bitterness, hostility, quick temper, contempt, violence, sarcasm, cynicism, constant irritability, put-downs and getting even.

Some people almost radiate waves of anger. An encounter leaves you wondering what you did to make them mad. A frown is their everyday attire, they address others abruptly, take offense at nothing, insult you without provocation ("Doctor, I want you to know I don't think much of psychologists!"), and search hard for reasons to complain. They may verbalize resentment toward spouses, coworkers, authority figures, family members and, often, toward God.

But anger can show another face. Some chronically angry people react just the opposite. They may act ingratiating, sweet, ultra-cooperative and pleasant. For instance, they may say, "Whatever you want to do is just fine with me. I'm willing to do anything!" But they don't mean a word of it. They may get even with you for choosing to do something they expect you to know *not* to do. Some of these folks smile nearly all the time no matter what's going on, because they've learned to mask their anger, which they themselves believe to be dangerous and sinful. Rarely explosive, they will betray their inner state by displaying "soft" signs of anger.

Soft signs of anger. Buried anger is one of the most common problems among Christians. For those who have repressed their anger at man or God, the first evidence of it may appear as stress or fatigue *not* related to physical exertion. Other indicators are:

"Getting even" with others by small, unobtrusive maneuvers. Are you deliberately late because your friend made you wait for her the last time you got together? Do you sit silently through the next hymn because the pastor never picks any of the hymns you've requested? Do you artfully slip the barest hint of chill into your voice because your son has overlooked your birthday? Do you stop yourself from doing a favor for somebody because you remember that person hasn't done anything for you lately?

Feeling irritable, agitated, restless, easily aggravated. You feel as though someone is constantly scratching a blackboard. You want to (but rarely do) fly off the handle with spouse, children, roommate, fellow employees, even your boss.

Physiological disorders. Elevated blood pressure, tense, aching muscles, headache, backache, cramps, spasms, high cholesterol, digestive complaints, spastic colon, ulcer, irritated bowel syndrome and even heart disease (according to some recent experiments) can spring from undealt-with anger.[1]

---

[1] All of these complaints may have other causes, so be certain your physician has ruled out medically treatable disorders. And even if your problem is anger, you may need to treat its physical symptoms as well.

Reaction to religion. Buried anger may surface in a reaction to religious words, phrases, or teachings. A person may even feel irritated, sad, or despairing when he hears the promises of God repeated. God's name, prayer, and the Word of the Lord may act as an abrasive and may provoke nit-picking arguments or expressions of cynicism.

Any or all of these symptoms may occur when we repress anger, despite God's promises that His children will enjoy the peaceable, joyful fruit of His Spirit (see Galatians 5:22, 23), and that His work in us will bring reconciliation with others (see 2 Corinthians 5:18).

Doubts . . . Distance . . . Meaninglessness. "God seems far away," Olive muttered. This sixty-five-year-old woman had suddenly lost her health, her husband of forty years, her home, her furniture and possessions and then one of her children. Antidepressant medication was not helping. She doubted God and was angry at Him because of what she perceived as His mistreatment of her. All this, in her eyes, deprived her life of meaning.

When we perceive God as malevolent and unpredictable, or withdrawn—despite everything His self-revelation in Christ Jesus tells us—we can become sick in mind, emotions and body. The resultant signs may be troublesome doubts and the sense that life is empty, even though God clearly promises to give us hope and a future (see Jeremiah 29:11).

Rationalizing bad choices. Symptoms of the rift with God can include *defenses* as well as feelings—for instance, rationalizing a choice that's bad.

When you or I want to indulge some sinful lust, it's easy to rationalize. Have you ever caught yourself saying, "I'm entitled to some enjoyment, even if it goes against God's commandments"?

Recently a man told me he was living with his girlfriend

because "I don't want to be burdened with a marriage I can't walk away from if things don't go right." He did not see his own confusion about the fact that real, true love always contains commitment. So the best he could come up with was a sad rationalization for his actions.

How sad that we can look for intimacy, acceptance, love—when all the time our *unsound* thinking keeps us from having the very thing we long for (see Proverbs 4:20—5:23).

Alcohol and drugs. When the rift with God leaves your life without *His* meanings, you will try to find that "lift" from another source.

As I've said earlier, I once tried to find meaning in alcohol. So I know that people who rely on chemicals find the drugs do offer a "high" that invariably works its deceptive magic. They really *believe* (though they may not be aware of it) that the chemical will do more for them than God can. Even their self-talk includes frequent references to their favorite intoxicant because they've come to believe it's their only way to endure life. So at three o'clock each afternoon, they'll remind themselves: "Only two hours, and I'll be able to have a drink. Life will be good again."

Many walk this route of substance abuse, seeking life but finding only more pain and alienation—ignoring both God's warnings and His offering of real life through union with the Holy Spirit (see Proverbs 20:1; Ephesians 5:18).

Loss of natural gratitude. Even dogs "smile" and wag their tails to thank you for some kindness. But rarely do people who have a rift with God experience inner impulses of gratitude toward Him, even if they identify themselves as Christians. Moreover, they rarely have an optimistic outlook about anything, and rarely see how God is active in their lives. Gradually, as the rift widens, they come to see the cause of good things as *chance,* and God as the source of bad things. Slowly *self* becomes the center of the universe.

Natural gratitude is normal and occurs instinctively in all human beings, not just in Christians. Examining the internal monologues of people who have a rift with God reveals a marked deficit in the instinctive response of a creature to his Creator's benevolence (see Psalms 65:11–13; 69:34; 96:11–13; 98:4–9).

Unmitigated self-centered expectations. Watch for conversation that reveals God has been pushed to a peripheral position. "Because I don't like it . . ." is sufficient reason why something should not happen. "I prefer to think . . ." is their best reason why reality should conform to their views. "I want it . . ." is adequate to explain why the universe owes them something.

In my own case, I wanted my family restored and refused to believe God could possibly do otherwise. After all, my demand was one hundred percent scriptural! God had no business *not* to perform according to my desires. I wanted it *my* way or no way. And I have frequently encountered similar self-centered demands in people suffering from the rift after a loss they feel is unjustified. All that self-centeredness can do is to close people into a dream world in which their *wants* have grown rampant as a jungle—even though Jesus declared that the one who loves and obeys Him will be greatly loved by the Father (John 14:23).

Distress because your world view is not working. In some people, you hear distress over the fact that their world view isn't working for them. They once figured life out and came up with some external function that they *thought* would make them happy and fulfilled—like position, success, fame, achievement, money, security, sex, or even "ministry for the Lord." They built their life's systems around this chosen view. But false gods always fail. The distress comes because they're afraid to forsake their god (whatever it may be), even though it has ceased to give them any pleasure.

What these folks must learn is how to rest in God and completely trust Him for their own sense of well-being and "place" in this world. They have leaned upon their own understanding of life, rather than drawing understanding from God (see Proverbs 3:5–8).

Cynicism. The cynic believes things can only get worse, never better. His gods have failed him, so why hope for the future, only to be let down again? Because zeal irritates cynical people, they show contempt for those who go around proclaiming they've been saved, healed, provided for or loved. The attitude is "Just *wait.*" He disdains emotion in religious settings.

Inside, he is frightened of exposing himself to another disillusioning let-down. The last thing he wants is another offering of hope. The only defense he can find is to view life as a question mark, and hold all hopeful answers in contempt.

But God says to the cynic: *You must trust me with all of your heart, soul, mind and strength—for when you cast the weight of your belief upon me fully, you'll find that I am the fulfillment of all things* (see Matthew 22:27). *Though all men may be liars, I am true* (see Romans 3:3, 4).

Fake religiosity with legalism. Religiosity is a psychological symptom, although it is rarely dealt with in psychological texts.[2] These are defenses adopted by some to paper over the rift with God.

---

[2]Psychology texts usually avoid religion, despite the fact that religion has major importance for most people. A few psychologists have produced excellent research on religious phenomena. Most, however, assume that religious issues are insignificant and need not be discussed in texts on abnormal psychology, psychotherapy, and personality theory. True, many psychologists are irreligious, but their assumption that therefore religion merits no careful consideration amounts to little more than an enormous bias.

The "religious" defense enables rift sufferers to avoid confronting the unpleasant truth about how far they have drifted, thus preserving a certain comfort—one that's purchased at a steep price.

"Super-spirituality" (which has nothing to do with the Holy Spirit) means maintaining an unearthly float in public but coming to earth in private with that chronic headache, addiction to alcohol or prescription drugs, or hunger for pornography. Fanatical or fraudulently "gung-ho" religious posturing may be accompanied by a very different hidden life of sadness, disappointment, failure and dishonesty. By their own timid, anxious cowering in safe, fake goody-goodness, some attest to the fear of missing their own perfectionistic standard.

Tranquilizers. Although abuse of alcohol and street drugs often accompanies the growing rift among some, prescription drugs are more often chosen to ease the pain of the religious person's life of hypocrisy. Valium and Xanax have their place in medical usage, but they can be abused, as can sleeping pills, tranquilizers, over-the-counter cold and pain medicines and cough syrups. Because these substances temporarily numb an anxious body, they can be used as aids in self-deception.[3] Sometimes, too, people who abuse medications spend a great deal of time in bed during the day. This may also be an escape or avoidance behavior, which, like depending on numbing chemicals, should force our attention back to the rift itself.

Defended *against* outward exposure and inner revelation of the truth, the legalist or super-fake-religious person misses out on the cleansing insight afforded by gen-

---

[3]But not *always.* I write this section with trepidation because there are many whose avoidance of *truly helpful* medication can be as perfectionistic and wrong-thinking as dependence on tranquilizers, *et al.* Certain psychotropic medications, far from merely deadening pain, *do* correct pathological, chemical imbalances. As always in life, it's important to discriminate.

uine spirituality. He resists seeing that his true adversary is his own rift-making sinful nature, which would be the first step toward health. Only when the sufferer faces this unpleasant and unwelcome truth—that there is still a God-defying nature within—can genuine spirituality begin its life-changing work.

"I Know A 'Friend' Who . . ."

Whom did you think of as you read the preceding diagnostic signs? Someone else? The morning I preached my first sermon as a young pastor, one family friend shook my hand and said, "I wish Sadie had been here. She really needed to hear that!" The danger is that you won't focus inward and allow God's Holy Spirit to shine His searchlight on symptoms of your own rift syndrome. It is so easy for each of us to rationalize and bury not only our anger but our other undesirable traits, too. So we say things like:

"I'm not depressed. I *can't* be. I'm trying to be a joyful Christian!"

"Anxious? Not me. Philippians tells us to 'have no anxiety about anything.' I'm a Bible-believing Christian. I can't be anxious."

"I'm not addicted to these tranquilizers. I *need* them!"

"Me—an alcoholic? No way! My Christian liberty allows me to have a drink now and then, but I can quit whenever I want to. Oh sure, I drink a little too much sometimes. Doesn't everybody?"

"I'm not being sarcastic. Can't anybody ever take a joke around here?"

"All my irritability is strictly due to my PMS."

"I'm frustrated because of my wife."

"I'm angry because of my chintzy employer and his cheap attitude. He never pays me enough for all the hard work I do!"

Why not ask the Lord of truth to show you those areas

where you may be manifesting the signs of the rift. Since He is never against us and only, always *for* us (see Romans 8), what can it hurt? Facing your symptoms is the first step toward diagnosis and cure.

How many of the following symptoms are characteristic of you? Use this checklist as a spiritual "mirror":

_____ I am frequently troubled with depression, discouragement and feeling that life is not worthwhile.

_____ I feel anxiety or dread about things I really shouldn't have to fear. For example:

    _____ I get anxious about what others might think of me.

    _____ I worry a lot about finances, health, the safety of people I love.

    _____ I feel tense and anxious about something, but I can't really pin down what it is.

_____ I get angry too often at _____ .

    _____ I am *chronically* angry at _____ .

_____ I try to get even with others in subtle, passive ways (for example, being late for appointments, doing or saying things I know they don't like).

_____ I think I carry around some buried anger.

_____ I have a quick temper.

_____ I'd like to hurt someone when I get mad.

_____ I get violent and hit people or break things.

_____ I know I'm mad at God because He did/didn't

_____ .

_____ I feel far away from God most of the time.

_____ I have the ability to come up with excuses and "reasons" for most of my faults and bad habits.

_____ I use alcohol and/or drugs, and I think I am dependent on one of these substances. (For instance, I occasionally drink too much; or, I couldn't get along without tranquilizers or sleeping pills.)

_____ If I am going to express gratitude to God, I have to fake it. (Or, I seldom express gratitude to God.)

_____ I almost never see things in an optimistic or positive light.

_____ I think of myself first, last, and always. Let other people worry about themselves.

_____ I think everyone I know is out for himself. You can't really trust anybody in this dog-eat-dog world.

_____ I put up a religious front so others will think I'm better than I am.

_____ I sometimes tell myself the following misbeliefs. (The following are misbeliefs especially indicative of a rift with God. If you find them in your self-talk often, it may indicate a serious spiritual problem):

_____ God often seems very far away.

_____ I think that God doesn't love me.

_____ God likes to see me suffer.

_____ Nothing works for me.

_____ Nothing changes when I pray.

_____ When I read the Bible, I get sad because none of the good in it applies to me.

_____ It's hard for me to believe that a good God would permit so much suffering.

_____ I've tried everything, with little or no emotional improvement.

_____ I frequently doubt God's existence, His goodness, or His promises.

_____ I find myself asking, "Why do I have all the *rotten* luck?" I think it's wrong of God to permit such awful things to happen to me all the time.

Diagnose Yourself

If you've honestly faced yourself in the mirror, it's time to make a diagnosis. But be careful: Most of us have been influenced by popular psychology to diagnose our maladies in terms of external problems, *not* spiritual malaise.

As a result, we usually allow surface symptoms to mask the deeper illness. Though gaining insight about the past can be a step toward deeper truth, it is only a step. So don't be content, for instance, with believing that the reason you're anxious or angry is that you were raised in a home where tempers were short. Don't rest with the conclusion that you get even by indirect tactics because you've always been terrified of letting anyone experience your anger directly. Move beyond the psychological to the spiritual.

This chapter was designed to show how various troubles relate to a hidden rift with the Lord. If you found, as you reviewed the checklist, that you resonate with some of the problems described, it's time to take the next step, which is the most critical of all.

Ask yourself: "Have I drifted or walked or run away from Him in some way? Do I have a problem with God *himself*?"

If you think perhaps you have, you will want to learn more about why it is so, and how to end a separation in which you can only lose. Don't your own symptoms—the bad fruit that can come when you are *dis*connected from God—bear witness to that?

Asking for Insight

Just before we go on to examine your response to God himself, I urge you to pray, in words like these:

Father, quicken my spirit by the power of your Holy Spirit. Lead me to know the truth about myself. If I have created a rift between you and me, please reveal it to me now and guide me toward healing. As I move deeper on this spiritual journey, reveal to my heart attitudes about you that are wrong and are causing any distance between us. I ask this through Jesus Christ, your Son. Amen.

Canoe Trip

BAD WEATHER

Three days of wind and rain
Three days of battling the waves
    and carrying wet packs
       from lake to lake.

Wet feet,
    wet firewood,
       wet and muddy tents,
          and tempers wearing thin.

But God, we asked for sunny skies,
    and gentle mirror lakes!
       And yet the heavens weep with us
        three days and nights,
       and then,
          the sun.

No, in all these things
    we are more than conquerors
       through him
        who loved us

FIVE

Is God Wrong About the Good?

Previously, we've looked at the ways we're affected by denial—that is, denial of feelings both toward ourselves and toward God. Beyond that, we've begun to take a realistic look at the symptoms plaguing us to see how they relate to the real root problem, which is the fact that we have somehow distanced ourselves from God.

Now we need to look at the nature of the rift itself. At the core of our problems, whatever shape they may take, I believe there lies one major issue: a disagreement with God over what is *good* and, specifically, what is good for you and me.

Whether we take issue with Him about something we want to do (that He's forbidden), or we object to some event in our lives we just don't want to accept (that He's allowed), our main belief is that God is wrong about what is best for us. It may surprise or disturb you, but misery over unpleasant events, or choosing to do wrong—both have their roots in the same argument with God.

The tragic story of Glenn and Kara illustrates my point.

Anatomy of a Rift With God

Kara had known it would be hard, but it was worse than she'd imagined. She'd given Glenn the "good news"—and now his face was flushing with anger. "Tell me you're making it up!" he responded. "Tell me you're not pregnant again."

"It's true," she replied, drawing on her courage. "The doctor couldn't believe it either. But I'm due in March. Please, Glenn, don't—"

"Don't *what*?" he interrupted angrily. "Don't get upset? Well, I *am* upset, Kara. I'm fifty-three years old. I've paid for three kids to go to college already. I want something out of life for *me* now. Kara—I want you to have an abortion."

"Glenn," she fired back, "you *know* I can't kill our child! I'm not thrilled about this either. But it's a fact we have to face. We can make it together."

"*I* don't have to face it," he said coldly.

A week later, Glenn was still adamant. He leveled an ultimatum. "Make up your mind, Kara. Either you get an abortion or you're on your own. I mean it. If you go through with this pregnancy, I leave."

Over the next unsettling month, the only words that passed between them were things like, "You'll need to have the car serviced today," or "I'll have dinner ready at six." Kara tried to hide her grief, and kept praying Glenn would calm down and accept the pregnancy. Glenn remained stony.

On a Sunday afternoon, Glenn dropped his bombshell: "I've decided, Kara, that whether or not you keep this baby, I'm entitled to find fulfillment in life somewhere, somehow. I want to find a little happiness before my life gets away from me and I end up bitter and disappointed. I'd rather take a beating than cause you pain—but I have to do what's best for *me*. That's the bottom line."

By the end of the week, Glenn had moved out. And Kara cried herself to sleep each night.

As for Glenn, he continued to tell himself he had every right to start an "adventurous" tryst with a woman in his office. Though he believed he was a Christian, Glenn told himself God would just have to understand how important it was for him to find "real" love and happiness. He couldn't quite believe that God understood his deep needs,

though, and that irritated him. So the disagreement between Glenn and God turned on the issue of the good.

Glenn rejected God's good on two different but related
counts.

First, Glenn rejected God's good by giving in to disappointment and anger over Kara's pregnancy. Glenn
formed a misbelief that he was "bound" to an aging, pregnant woman, which meant that his lot in life was terrible.
The pregnancy was wholly unacceptable because his marriage had lost its physical allure.

But you see, Glenn's marriage and Kara's pregnancy
were both circumstances God had either determined or
permitted. By believing false notions about the importance of feeling "in love," and by telling himself that ex-
citement and freedom from responsibility were the ultimate good, Glenn chose to believe that God was *wrong* for
going "against" him.

Second, Glenn went on to reject God's good by acting
contrary to what God has declared to be good. Dumping
his responsibility for wife and family, Glenn made a choice
to do what he believed was good for him. Glenn went his
own way—which was *away* from God.

Maybe, as a Christian, you cannot identify with
Glenn's sin or his choice to turn away from God. But *stop.*
Doesn't every conscious choice to disobey God or to blame
God carry us away from Him? We must be careful we do
not become like the Pharisee who looked at the "sinner"
and said, "Thank God I'm not like that man." That kind
of self-righteous attitude is *blindness,* and carries us onto
the most dangerous ground where we become deadened
to the Holy Spirit's convicting nudges as He puts His finger
on our sins.

When we disagree with God, or resist Him, aren't we
really saying, "I know that's good for *me.* I know what I
need"? Even Christians can take the stance that we know
what's good for us personally most of the time. Sure, we
readily admit we don't know *everything,* but somehow we

believe we know our own needs. That's because we've accepted the fallacy that what we *want* is a reliable index of what we *need*. So we equate wants with what's good for us.

In other words, if I want something, it's bound to be good. And if God thinks otherwise, then I have a quarrel with Him. I'm even willing to doubt God's love and wisdom when I don't get what I want.

What you and I are too willing to say is that God is *wrong*.

Let's further explore what happens in a relationship where there is a big disagreement.

When I argue with another person it's because I'm quite sure I know what's right and the other person doesn't. The trouble is, the other person is just as certain that he knows exactly what's right and good. As a result we move apart.

During the past few days in my consulting room, I've listened to several instances of this struggle over the good, which mars and ruins so many human relationships:

Trish complains because Greg insists on playing golf three days a week, while she wants him focused totally on their small business. For him, golf is good, while tending to business is a drag. And for Trish, having Greg apply himself to business is good, while his golf is pointless and getting the family nowhere.

Harold rehearses an argument with his mother over marijuana. She wants him to quit using the drug, while Harold believes moderate use helps him relax. Harold argues that his marijuana smoking is good, while his mother argues that he must quit.

Ruth recounts a discussion with her pastor about women taking part in the worship service. "I told him the time has come to include women among the worship leaders, but he won't listen. He keeps saying that the Bible never tells us women can lead worship. He is so exasperating!"

Phil tells of his son's contention that he is too old and too slow to work in the family business, so he should retire. Phil claims that he knows the ropes from long experience and is therefore too valuable an asset for the business to lose.

Cindy bewails the fact that her husband wants to use their extra income to build a nest egg, while she wants to make needed repairs on the house. They argue endlessly.

Do you see how each contender in these arguments believes his or her idea will result in the highest good? It's easy to argue without ever addressing to the other person's point when you and your "opponent" have different perspectives. You can begin to appreciate how—despite the conundrums posed for the human race by the question of "good"—you and I think our view is right, even when God thinks otherwise.

Think back to Glenn, who resented his wife's late-in-life pregnancy. Glenn believed, like many other people, that his own immediate satisfaction was the highest good. In the light of this "certainty," he left Kara and their unborn child for someone else. In fact, Glenn distorted the truth until it was no longer true, until he called "evil good and good evil" (see Isaiah 5:20). To say it bluntly, he had perverted his sense of good until he was fully on the side of wrong.

Even well-intentioned, spiritual people can miss God's good plan for them, as so many men and women in the Bible demonstrate. David thought it would be good to get rid of Bathsheba's husband, Uriah, to cover his own sin of adultery. James and John and their mother, Salome, thought they were wise to ask for first-rank positions in Jesus' coming kingdom. Ananias and Sapphira thought it would be good to withhold a financial cushion for themselves and lie about it to the apostles. Peter thought it would be good not to eat with Gentiles in front of some Jewish emissaries from James. Though each one thought he knew how to choose the good, he was wrong.

This confronts us with a great irony; we see the anatomy of our rift with God: The reason we choose options that are clearly forbidden by God is *not* that we think these things will be bad for us. We do so because we believe they will be good! And we wind up complaining about Him, even angry at Him, because He has forbidden things that ruin us and point us in the direction of life, health and blessing!

Consider it: People don't soak their brains in alcohol or take pills because they believe something bad will come of it, but because they're sure they'll find pleasure. We don't lie, cheat, commit adultery, or gossip because we think we'll suffer, but because we think we'll find what our hearts desire. And so we consciously turn away from God because we think we know what's best for us. Our sin-clouded minds have decided that our Creator and His laws are all wrong!

Man's Finite Mind Contends With the Mind of God

Thus far, we've been considering the two main forms our disagreements with God take: First, we often object to what God does or what He allows to happen to us; second, we make choices He has forbidden. But we have not yet mentioned the most common term for a dispute with God: It's called sin.

Psychologically understood, sin roots and begins to grow when my finite mind contends with God, telling me that God is wrong about which choices and actions are good for me. When I have decided God *is* wrong, then I act on my own judgment, in opposition to God. In that sense, sin is as much a psychological aberration as hysteria or depression, springing from that dark corner of the mind where false beliefs reign.

Unlike the sometimes glamorous pictures people paint for themselves of sin—clever men in pin-striped suits hatching foolproof schemes for getting rich, sexy bodies intertwined in slim-lined tangles, exciting beverages bubbling in cocktail glasses, frolic, thrills, high living—the *reality* is that sin is not glamorous—sin ends in death.

The Oprah Winfrey Show once featured a guest who knew a great deal about deliverance from evil spirits, a priest-author-exorcist, Malachi Martin. Looking for all the world like a mischievous leprechaun, Father Martin arched his eyebrows, peered straight into the camera, and whispered, "Oprah, the *mind* is where Satan wants to get you. The *mind!* The devil isn't going to jump out from behind a bush and grab you. He doesn't aim at your glands to snare you. He goes for your *mind!* Your *mind,* Oprah! And if he can get your mind, he's got *you!*" The way Malachi said the word *mind* made you uneasy enough to glance back over your shoulder just in case the shadow you saw out of the corner of your eye *was* something moving toward you. Nobody watching that show would ever forget the point: Your mind is your most vulnerable organ.

I believe Malachi Martin was right. When Satan can mess with your mind, he will try to persuade you that God has made a mistake about the good. That error is the fountainhead of evil. Therefore, sin does not grow out of our appetite for food or drink. It doesn't originate in our genitals. It can't be caused by wealth or good looks, or by other people dangling tempting trinkets before our eyes. We don't sin because friends "make" us envy, or do things that grate. Sin originates in my mind and yours when we accept the idea that something is good which God has declared bad, or when we consider as bad that which God has called good. At that moment, we have opened up a rift with God.

Since Eve holds the unfortunate distinction of creating the first rift with God, which led to the first sin, let's pay close attention to her story for a moment. It will help us to know how critical a mental rift with God is in the process that leads to sin.

Eve apparently had two beliefs fixed in her mind from the beginning: (1) life, health and blessing came from obedience to the Creator; (2) doing what God had forbidden would bring death. She knew that what God willed for her was only good.

Enter Satan, who messed with Eve's mind by what we'd call a "consciousness-raising, educational discussion." By allowing herself to entertain the Enemy's suggestion that maybe God wasn't as good as He seemed, Eve came away believing that the one thing in the world God had denied was truly good for her.

Imagine Eve's revised self-talk: She must have told herself that the luscious-looking fruit would do her so much good God would be threatened by her. And when she acquired that wonderful knowledge of good and evil—what could possibly keep her from being like God?

It was, as they say, heady stuff. True, it would cost something, but the good results seemed worth the risk. She had to change her mind, to adopt the entirely novel premise (novel at that point in human history, but quite common today) that God's command was a lie. Then there was no reason *not* to eat it. Adam, too, was convinced, and what took place in their minds was the initial rift, which led to disobedience and sin, followed by the consequence: death.

If we want to defeat the power of sin, you and I must learn to ferret out the deep, deep error of believing God is wrong, ridding our minds of every tendency to dispute Him, and filling our minds with the truth. Filling our minds with right beliefs founded on God's Word is precisely what the Bible means by "growing in faith," and it is the only road to success in overcoming the power of sin.

Beliefs That Generate Sin

For any one of us to come to the point of believing that wrong is right and God is bad, we have to adopt certain notions. They're shocking, really, when you stop to examine them:

God's will for me and His commands are what's best for Him, not for me. His insistence that I obey Him only springs from a tyrannical heart, or an egotistical need to be in control.

If God's commands are not best for me, then He must be lying to His own advantage. He cannot be trusted. I can never be sure God wills the good for me, especially if it appears that my good might diminish Him, or interfere with a plan of His, or limit His control over me.

Even if God doesn't come right out and lie about the good, He might be wrong about what's good for me. It doesn't matter whether God lies or simply doesn't *know* what's good for me as well as I do. I am now in the position of God.

Therefore, I will have to decide for myself what the good is. I can't rely on anybody. I'm the only one I can trust. I'm the final arbiter of my own good. The accompanying truth I must now face is terrifying: I am alone; and mistakes can be worse than fatal.

Eve's Offspring

Does any of this prove that sin works the same way in every instance? Scripture seems to indicate it does.

Jesus, in His famous teaching on the source of sin, said, "Out of the heart come evil thoughts" (Matthew 15:19). Scholars indicate the term *heart* means the same thing as *mind*. St. Paul also used the term *mind* to teach

how sinful living comes from wrong believing and thinking, while right living comes from setting your *mind* on a
godly train of thought (see Romans 8:3–7).

Let's examine this more closely.

Every sin is acted out of a belief. The same is also true—
though it sounds like a hard saying—of every unhappiness. When I refused to accept my unhappy circumstances, alone and homeless, I chose instead to believe
God had allowed evil to ruin me and, therefore, He was in
the wrong. I started to abuse and misuse alcohol and other
people's love. Since I had learned to distinguish right from
wrong long before, how could this be?

Here is how it happened: My mind became convinced
that God was wrong. Contrary to what He'd said about
such behavior, I believed it would be good for me to forget
my misery by numbing my brain and that I should take
love where I found it. Because of my pitiable circumstances and because God could hardly be trusted (seeing
that He'd betrayed my trust so badly), I felt I had to take
hold of the reins of my life. This sounds abhorrent (and
we don't usually spell it out this plainly), but if we have
the courage to look, we'll find that such misbeliefs regularly undergird our sins.

Take the client who described her ongoing affair with
a married man. "We're so in love," she said. "It *must* be
from God." At the same time, it was causing everyone,
herself included, so much pain. She was sorry about the
pain—so sorry. But she just could not let go of the affair,
though she, too, was married. She bought into the erroneous belief that pleasant sensations must be meeting important needs and are therefore good. ("I'm starved for
romance, Doctor. And his wife never gives him any support.") She also told herself that God must understand her
need for "true love." In time He would come around in
sympathy with her pursuit of this counterfeit "good." If
only everyone could just work through the pain!

Take another example—the college student who was

plagued with fear, doubt and guilt. He told me, "I did copy just one answer from the guy in front of me, because I *need* that graduate fellowship," he reasoned. "And to get it, I have to earn top grades. Why should one stupid question stand in my way?" This man had twisted the strands of his mind into a tangle of truth and error, with the result that he could excuse his own wrongdoing.

Let's take another approach now. Let's look at some obvious sins that we, Eve's offspring, fall into, and trace back to their root cause:

Consider the sin of *pride.* Many people believe this trait contains the raw material from which all sins are made, because in it I make myself god. If I go to the heart of my sinful pride, I come to the belief that position, others' admiration and attention are essential to my life and well-being. I just can't buy Jesus' statement that my good lies in becoming a humble, lowly servant. He must be mistaken, or lying, because getting attention and having my own way *feel* so good.

Envy can be defined as the misbelief that it's best to prevail over others. Unless my possessions or status are greater than those of others, I can't be happy. I believe that Jesus drifted off into unworkable romanticism when He contended that my highest good comes from seeking the good of others.

Greed is the misbelief that the highest good lies in owning things purely for the sake of possessing them. This contradicts the wisdom of Jesus, who said that "a [person's] life does not consist in the abundance of his possessions" (Luke 12:15).

Anger (the deadly sin, not the mere emotion of anger) comes from the misbelief that revenge is good and that it's stupid to forgive.

Gluttony consists not in eating or drinking too much occasionally but in the abiding error that consumption is the answer to most of life's problems. So when you're feeling down, the only answer is to down a half gallon of ice cream or to "shop till you drop."

When a Christian sins, he begins with misbeliefs just like anyone else. They lead him to perform actions that are contrary to God.

Unfortunately, most of us have also bought into another misbelief: "It's okay for me to sin *once in a while*—to hang on to 'little' sins that I do all the time—even if it hurts others or myself. I'm forgiven, so the consequences won't be that bad." But the Bible says that the "fruit" of every sinful activity is *death.*

Adam and Eve didn't stop breathing the moment they ate the forbidden fruit—but they died. Death is first of all spiritual. It's the state of trying to exist apart from God, dragging along without His fellowship, pulling your own weight without His help, of trying to sink the roots of your spirit—which are shriveling—into things that do not, *cannot* give life. And finally, it's having your heart quit beating and your soul go on to face a permanent state of separation from God. Ultimately, sin is not just our pulling away from God, not just insisting He must be wrong and we must be right. There comes a point where God will say, "My Spirit will not contend with man forever" (Genesis 6:3). This is a frightening state to come to.

God, having done all He can to reach across the rift with His loving arms, will, at some point, turn from us if we do not turn to Him first. This is a state we do not read about too often, even (unfortunately), in too many "popular" Christian books: It is the state of damnation.

I hasten to say this is *not* what God wants for His children. And He will always take us back if we return and agree with Him. But it's true that by pulling away repeatedly, by practicing the habit of second-guessing God, by rehearsing the "God-is-wrong" misbeliefs until they're habitual, we make the rift wider and deeper until it is a hardened, nerveless scar on our soul that can no longer sense the difference between wrong and right.

Perhaps by seeing sin and death for what they are, we can best grasp the decisive importance of *beliefs* and the thoughts that follow from them in the *mind*. In the Bible, it's a signature theme. In a dozen different ways, the Scriptures say it is *beliefs* that create feelings and galvanize us into actions, bad or good, the end result being death or life. (Some examples are Isaiah 26:3; Lamentations 3:21; Matthew 22:37; Mark 14:72; Luke 12:29; Romans 1:28. Especially note Romans 8:5, 7 and 12:2.)

And now—great surprise!—contemporary psychology and the Bible sing this theme in close harmony. Arriving through scientific research at the very conclusion God has laid bare in Scripture, cognitive psychologists have learned that what you believe and how you believe it determine the emotions you feel and the actions you perform. Wrong beliefs, or as I have labeled them, *misbeliefs*, no matter how sincere, generate wrong behavior, disagreeable emotions and *bondage* because they are contrary to what God has revealed.

Do you and I know what's good for us? Sometimes. But when we disagree with God—when we call bad things good and go after them—we are like dogs returning to their own vomit because they think it tastes good (see 2 Peter 2:22). Life itself often proves us totally wrong when we argue with God over the good.

Is the Good Different From What I Thought?

Is it possible that the *good* for me is something different, even far different, from what I have ever imagined? What about circumstances beyond my choosing that are painful? That issue, though not altogether different than the issue of moral decisions, does remain. Let's introduce it here, then examine it more closely in subsequent chapters.

Because Christianity offers pure truth, it can make us psychologically healthy. That means Christianity must be full of surprises, and I have had just enough life experience to say this is so. On the issue of the good, I can expect Christianity to upend my assumptions, and give them a sharp whack. Not only is the good different than what I often assume, but the spiritual and emotional problems I've had with accepting my circumstances can also be traced to misbeliefs about good.

I now ask you to consider: Is it possible that the *good* can sometimes be so different from what we think that it can even be the very thing we have called "bad"?

If that sounds shocking or offensive, it may be an indication of how much of the world's "wisdom" and independence we've bought into. Sometimes the good may be what hurts, deprives, or disappoints us. Jesus' crucifixion, Paul's thorn in the flesh, the shedding of the martyrs' blood—all appeared bad, to the point that the devil got enthusiastic about sponsoring them. But God knew how to use those evils, turning them into good—*surprising* good, good so different from what anyone thought that nobody could have imagined it. Jesus' death led to His resurrection and *ours,* Paul's thorn became a minister preventing self-reliance, and the martyrs' blood was the seed of the church.

Are you willing to take a deeper look? To consider that your inner difficulties might be due to erroneous assumptions about the good? That getting well, or solving your problems, or arriving at a state of wholeness, or "making it"—whatever the goal may be—depends on letting go of your misbeliefs? In the next two chapters, we are going to examine two bedrock issues, issues upon which the course of your life and spiritual well-being depend: Does God *really* allow only good to come my way? Have I replaced Him, at the core of my soul, with a false god I consider to be my highest good?

Canoe Trip

FIRST CAMPSITE

Long, flat rock,
Just right for beaching our canoes.
There we sat down and wept,
    as we remembered
        husband and father
           gone forever
                where we cannot follow
                now.

And Jim, our friend,
not knowing how to comfort us,
threw out a line from shore,
    and caught one great big fish,
        yelling for us to come
           and bring a landing net.

How strange to catch a fish
    right here,
        without live bait,
           without half trying,
               just casting aimlessly.

And so we dried our tears
    and laughed together,
        built a fire
           and fried our fish
           for breakfast.

By the waters of Babylon,
    there we sat down and wept,
        when we remembered
        Zion.

Jesus said to them,
    "Come and have breakfast."

SIX

The Point of Contention

"The word *good* has many meanings," wrote G. K. Chesterton. "For example, if a man were to shoot his grandmother at a range of five hundred yards, I should call him a good shot, but not necessarily a good man."

Chesterton was right in what he implied: The *good* is not always easy to define. Perhaps you, like most folks, have just assumed that *knowing* what's good is easy, and that obtaining a good life is the hard part. But it's really not that easy to know what's good *in a given situation*. Which circumstances will develop into good, and what choices are good for us may *not* be as clear as you've thought.

Why is it so important to explore this issue of what is good? Because at the core of every damaged emotion lies a mistaken assumption about what the good is. Yes, I'm saying we can actually make *ourselves* miserable by telling ourselves the good is something other than what God has given or allowed us. And, as we've seen, we set ourselves up to sin in precisely the same way, telling ourselves we know best what's good for us. I have never seen anybody's internal rift healed until he has grasped the surprising truth about the good with both hands. Do you want to get well? Be whole? Have a sound mind? Then take time to work through what we're about to undertake.

Why Do We Argue With God About Good?

My conviction is that our disagreements arise because of this issue—a general confusion over good. We use the

93

good to mean many things. Here is only a partial list of the various things we mean when we say something is good:

pleasant, clean, morally right, without sin, having a favorable outcome, amicable, well behaved, a thing worth striving for, advantageous, full of positive events, enjoyable, serviceable, in accord with accepted norms, high quality, appropriate, healthful, genuine, useful, kind, a possession, a quiet and beneficial effect, able, trustworthy, accurate, close, peaceful.

So when I say something is good for me, that may be true insofar as it includes one of those terms I've just listed.

Nevertheless, God knows—and we can come to understand if we are open—that not everything that's good for some purpose is therefore good for you or me. And not everything that's good for us at one time is good for us at another.

So it boils down to this: First, there are some good things God has willed for us to relinquish. When we insist on our "rights" and choose them anyway, it's sin. Second, there are other good things that He permits Satan, circumstances, or our own foolishness to take away, knowing He can still give us greater good things later. The exact reason _why_ may remain hidden. But when we persist in disagreeing, complaining and quarreling, we create a rift with our Maker, and this only aggravates our problem.

What makes the truth seem hard at times is that the thing we're holding on to can be a splendid creation of God that might even be good for us if kept in its proper place. For instance, let's say that a woman enjoys the humor and caring nature of a male co-worker, and in the right framework their friendship is a joy. But either one can pervert the relationship by believing that it would be good to turn it into an illicit affair.

Likewise, the good of material abundance can be perverted until we tell ourselves we must be surrounded by beautiful possessions in order to be happy. The person who would sell his soul for his house, automobile, boat, television, computer, or money in the bank has a twisted idea of good. Possessions become idols.

A good and sterling reputation can become so crucial that it seems you can't live without it. If you own that particular misbelief, you will not have a minute's peace until you can guarantee that everyone will always think well of you. So reputation becomes an idol.

When life destroys or threatens one of our idols, we say, "This is wrong. It shouldn't happen. God has failed me miserably." Then we freeze, emotionally and spiritually, refusing to let God turn evil into good. Feeling bad, we refuse to allow Him to work, thinking, "He can't be trusted," when the truth is, *we* are the covenant-breakers and idolaters.

Hold On a Minute . . .

Maybe you're asking, "Do I have to accept that everything God allows to happen is *good*? Is *everything* that befalls me good?"

I've had to struggle with those questions, too, during some painful times. My mother lay on her back in the hospital for seven months, suffering greatly before she died. As a Christian, do I have to say *that* is good? A friend put a gun in his mouth and pulled the trigger to end his life. Must his family find a way to call that tragedy good? An eleven-year-old boy is kidnapped and sexually abused by a perverted child molester, and later his body is found brutally disfigured. A family's home burns to the ground. A great religious leader is exposed as a crook. A plane crash claims two hundred forty-three lives. A baby is born brain-damaged beyond repair. Do we as Christians have to affirm that these things, in themselves, are good? Are we wrong to feel hurt or angry about them? Do we have to be dishonest about our emotions?

I don't believe we do. Injustice, pain and loss are not good *in themselves.* Evil is evil, and the Bible tells us that it is engineered by the devil. Some pseudo-Christian leaders and movements have denied that anything at all is evil, a concept made easier for many today to accept because of the rise of nature religions and eastern philosophies. Dostoyevsky's innocent child, shivering in the outhouse, suffering pain she did nothing to cause, truly gnaws at our hearts because we see absolute injustice and evil having their way. But the answer is not to call good evil, or to blur the image of God as revealed in Jesus Christ and in the Bible.

Just as a radiologist can cure disease with destructive radiation or a surgeon with burning laser beams, God *allows* the evil to happen and at the same time uses it as a sculptor's tool for His good purpose (see Isaiah 45:7). We have to insist that He knows what He is doing, that He is not unfair or unjust (see Revelation 15:3). He is not helpless to rescue and save even in the midst of a flood of evil (see Numbers 11:23; Psalm 98:1).

The truth is, the world has fallen into the lap of the wicked one for a time. When we believe distressing events *shouldn't* happen, we are believing in a fantasy. It is true that our prayers can create a way for God to act, and He always hears us (James 5:16). But God does tell us He will not always act *in the way we ask Him to act* because His ways are higher than ours (see Isaiah 55:8, 9). When we still insist on our own way, we're like a person who is slowly going blind. God's true light gets dimmer, while at the same time we imagine there is light coming from corners where there is only darkness.

You and I need a hand when it comes to knowing what *good* is. Left to ourselves, we run into problems. Here are some questions you might find yourself puzzling over. All are questions about the good, though they don't focus on circumstances. Instead, they raise the issue of the good in our *choices* and *actions*. All of them really ask what good is:

- Do I *have* to go to church if I'm to be a Christian?
- Is it wrong to drink alcohol?
- If I plan very carefully for the future, if I put away savings for my later years, does this mean I'm not trusting God sufficiently? Am I doing wrong?
- Do I have to be nice to a person who isn't nice to me?
- Is it right for us as a nation to be building all these nuclear bombs when they mean potential death for the human race and utter devastation to the earth?
- I wonder if I should be a computer programmer or a nurse. Which is right for me?
- We should be saving our money so our children can go to college, rather than spending it on pleasant vacations, shouldn't we?
- Isn't it good for you to let go completely sometimes and just do what you feel like?
- Shouldn't people be allowed to decide when they want to die?
- Women should be given control over their own bodies and an absolute right to decide whether to have abortions.
- If a Christian and a non-Christian are both running for office, you should always vote for the Christian.
- I've been feeling especially attracted to my pastor lately, and I think he likes me. Is it wrong to feel this way?

Each represents doubt or belief people harbor concerning what's good and what's bad. Some of these dilemmas will have an obvious line between right and wrong, good and bad, for readers. Others fall into the "it all depends" category. Yet, they're issues on which someone has to apply wisdom to come up with a decision. The point is, *whose wisdom do you apply?* Without God, we can generate dangerous choices, miss the good and fall into tremendous difficulty.

What Is the Truth I Should Tell Myself?

So Chesterton was right, in a *sense*. Good does have an elusive quality—but that is only true when we *start* at the point of our circumstances and try to work our way back to God. There is another way to approach life, though it's difficult for many to see it, since our culture has pumped us so full of its "me-first, me-only, man-centered" philosophies.

As the great Christian teacher Oswald Chambers puts it in his excellent book *Shade of His Hand,* Western thought begins with man and tries to figure out and judge God. Hebrew thought, however, begins with bedrock truth about God and applies that truth to man and his erring ways. It is the opposite of the way we think, and that reversed thinking is exactly what causes so many of us problems: We believe our thoughts and perceptions are right *regardless* of what the Word of God says!

As an exasperated client once told me, "But *my* misbeliefs are true!" She expressed something many people struggle with: What if you don't see the flaws in your arguments when you have a disagreement with God? What if you aren't sure when what you're telling yourself is falsehood or the truth?

I recommend, when you've come to that point, that you go back to the beginning—to the simple elemental truths.

Regardless of circumstances or feelings, what *should* you be planting in the core of your being instead of the misbeliefs that are presently generating discontent with life or sinful, harmful choices and actions?

Here are foundational stones of truth that you must be

sure to cement in place in your heart/mind/self-talk, replacing the misbeliefs about God that presently generate discontent, sin and harmful choices:

God is good. Do you tell yourself often, or do you suspect in your deepest heart, that God is not really good? When you believe: that God won't keep His promises or that He has broken them; that God doesn't love you; that God is trying to harass and make trouble for you; that He enjoys torturing you; that He isn't for you but against you, regardless of what He says—then you are really telling yourself God isn't good. Watch for misbeliefs like this:

"A God of love, goodness and justice wouldn't run a world where such terrible things happen."

"If God were truly good and caring, He wouldn't forbid me to do what I really want to do."

"Fine thing! Some God! Allowing things like this tragedy to happen to me."

"If God exists, He's a cruel sadist."

"God is mean."

"God doesn't do what He has said He will do in the Bible."

Here is truth you can use to combat such notions: *"God is light; in him there is no darkness at all"* (1 John 1:5). God's goodness sparkles and shines through everything He has made. You can see it in His creation of beauty and order, harmony and balance all over the universe (see Psalm 19). You can see it in His careful provision for the daily needs of every tiny creature (see Psalm 145:15). You can see it most of all in Jesus Christ, for in Him, God has come to earth to give himself totally to save His world. Such self-giving is nothing but pure goodness and all-out love. You can't look at the cross and think "God is unloving." Once you look at the cross, you can't look at anything else, no matter how horrid it appears, and infer that God's intention is to do us harm. The truth is that God is good, that whatever evil you find is not of His invention or doing, and that He has a good will toward you. He loves you.

As Psalm 25:8–10 says:

> Good and upright is the Lord; therefore he instructs sinners in his ways. He guides the humble in what is right and teaches them his way. All the ways of the Lord are loving and faithful to those who keep the demands of his covenant.

So drive the pain-creating misbeliefs out of your self-talk and stop giving them your support. Replace them with truth, like this: "I don't have to keep making myself miserable with the belief that God is uncaring, unloving, and evil, or that He can't possibly love me. The fact that bad things occur doesn't prove God is bad. I'm going to tell myself the truth. He is good, He loves me, and He is *for* me—no matter what happens. He won't let me go, so I'm not going to let go of Him."

God knows what's best. Are you telling yourself that you know better than God what's good for you? Maybe you think that since you live inside your skin and God doesn't, He may know the big picture but He doesn't know *your* feelings and deepest needs. His commands cannot apply to you, because He probably doesn't share your goals, or know exactly where you want to go in life. So even if His laws are, in general, "good principles," they don't apply to you. Or maybe you think God is too distant or too occupied with vast concerns to know you exist.

Do you fill your mind with thoughts like the following:

> "God's commandments are good as general principles, but when He wrote them, He didn't know exactly what would be best for me in this situation at this time."
>
> "I feel as if I'm kind of lost to God—as if He doesn't really know about me, doesn't have me on

His mind. After all, I'm pretty insignificant in the grand scale of things."

"God may know what's best for some people, but I'm different and I don't think He fully appreciates that it's best for me to do such and such (which His law has forbidden). If God only understood how important this is to me, I'm sure He'd let me do it."

"I wonder if God knows what He's doing. It looks to me as if He's made a mistake."

By telling yourself God doesn't know what you need, or doesn't know that you exist, or doesn't know what He's doing, you rob yourself of tremendous help. How can you feel anything but insecure, unsafe and unprotected if the God who runs the universe is a sleepy old man who's amiable enough, but is simply not "with it"? Or if you believe in a limited deity who is even now in the process of becoming wiser but who hasn't reached infinity yet? Believing these things can make you nothing but empty and searching all the time!

God does know you intimately, and He knows your needs (see Matthew 10:29–31). He knows every breath before you breathe it, every thought before you think it, every wish before you wish it, and every need before you need it. Not only does He know all your conscious thoughts, He knows even your unconscious mind—thoughts buried so deep you'll never be aware of them yourself. He knows you throughout your whole history—as a just-fertilized egg in the womb, through every moment of your particular past and on into your future. He knows your tomorrows, the hour of your death and your eternal future. Therefore He knows what's good for you. He knows how best to make use of the anguish and evil that happens to you and He knows best what good things to send or allow you. He knows what's best for you to choose and to do. Tell yourself the truth that God *knows*.

Psalm 147:4 tells us God is great enough that He "determines the number of the stars and calls them each by name." So challenge your misbeliefs and replace them with truth like this:

> O Lord, you have searched me and you know me. You know when I sit and when I rise; you perceive my thoughts from afar. You discern my going out and my lying down; you are familiar with all my ways. Before a word is on my tongue you know it completely, O Lord . . . my frame was not hidden from you when I was made in the secret place. When it was woven together in the depths of the earth, your eyes saw my unformed body. All the days ordained for me were written in your book before one of them came to be. (Psalm 139:1–4, 15, 16)

God is strong. He can help. Have you been undermining your confidence in God with the notion that when bad things happen to good people, God has lost control—that He is as surprised, stunned, dismayed and helpless as you are? Such a mindset arises out of misbeliefs like these:

> "God would like to do something about this situation, but He can't. The devil is in charge."
> "Human wills, being free, are too much for God. He can't do anything about it when people make wrong choices."
> "God is very powerful, but sometimes evil is stronger."
> "I feel as if the good in the world is losing to the bad."

Such thoughts or philosophies diminish God's power and do terrific damage. While they may appear to solve the puzzle of how evil things can happen in a world run by a good God, they create an even worse difficulty by causing us to rely on *ourselves.*

God is all-powerful. Nothing is too hard for Him. Whatever the reason for an evil occurrence, the truth is that

God *could* prevent such things from happening. He is big enough and strong enough so that by sheer force He can do anything. And God's position is *not* to stand idly by. He doesn't shrug it off, saying, "I can do nothing about this."

We may not know *why* God chooses not to prevent a particular evil event. We may not know why He chooses not to prevent us from making wrong choices. But we do know this: There is no evil too powerful for Him to deal with and no calamity that He cannot turn into sheer, unblemished good. By allowing His Son to be taken by wicked men, crucified and killed, suffering all that evil had to deal out, the Father did enough to solve the problem of evil and to set a course that will remove it from His world. And you and I will be there to experience the grand resolution—*if* we hang on to the truth (see Colosians 1:21–23).

So sponge out of your thoughts any doubts about God's ability to right all wrongs in His universe. Replace your doubts about His power, and plan with truth like this:

> "Jesus said, 'All authority in heaven and on earth has been given to me' " (Matthew 28:18).
>
> "And we know that in all things God works for the good of those who love him, who have been called according to his purpose. . . . If God is for us, who can be against us?" (Romans 8:28, 31).
>
> "I know that you [Lord] can do all things; no plan of yours can be thwarted" (Job 42:2).
>
> "Then the end will come, when [Jesus Christ] hands over the kingdom to God the Father after he has destroyed all dominion, authority and power. For he must reign until he has put all his enemies under his feet. The last enemy to be destroyed is death. For he 'has put everything under his feet.' Now when it says that 'everything' has been put under him, it is clear that this does not include God himself, who put everything under Christ. When he has done this, then the Son himself will be made subject to him who put everything under him, so

that God may be all in all" (1 Corinthians 15:24–28).

Do I Have to Know *Why*?

A young man came to me just after being told by his physician that he had a malignant tumor in his eye, a tough blow at age twenty-three. "Just tell me this, Doctor," the young man demanded of me, "*why* did God allow this to happen to me?"

In light of our discussion about misbeliefs, let's take a look at what we tell ourselves about our "right to know." Take some time to carefully consider whether one or more of the following attitudes may be yours:

> "God has an *obligation* to tell me *why*."
>
> "If I *don't* know why things happen as they do, then God has violated my rights as a citizen of this universe."
>
> "If He hasn't told me why, it means there's something He's keeping from me."
>
> "Only if I know and approve of God's plan can He proceed."
>
> "I don't understand why this has happened to me after all I've done to serve God. I've been a faithful Christian, born again, filled with the Holy Spirit, baptized, praying regularly, immersed in the Scriptures—so after all the other knocks and misfortunes I've had to stagger up from—*why*?"
>
> "Does God have it in for me? If He doesn't, He has a funny way of showing fairness—singling me out like this! Why *me*?"

Do you see what we do when we *demand* to know why? We usurp God's place. But God never speaks of His government as a democracy, subject to committees and votes. *His* is the kingdom, the power and the glory—and He is a benevolent Monarch.

It is interesting to me that so many people begin psychotherapy because they want to know why they believe or act in certain ways—as if by knowing *why*, we mortal men can change for the better the way things are. Self-knowledge is not the answer. Nor is demanding that we possess God's wisdom. Even if we had it, there would still be one big problem: You and I are not the infinite, loving, holy being we call *God*.

So knowing *why* is not the supreme good, despite the teeth-gnashings of us who are "rational" creatures. Sometimes God does speak to our hearts by the Holy Spirit to reveal an answer. Other times He doesn't give a reason, and no matter how hard we try, we can't come up with one. At such times, getting the truth into our hearts means accepting the truth that *you don't have to know why.* He can bring great good out of the worst evil without it making the least bit of sense to you; His commands are still right and true, even if you don't understand why He gave them.

The truth is, you and I don't have to know why. It's not essential to our learning to cope. What *is* essential is truth. Tell yourself truth, like this:

> Like Jesus, I have come to do the will of God (Hebrews 10:9). I will accept what God permits to happen and do what He commands whether I see the reason and purpose clearly or not. I may not know all the reasons but, as Scripture says, I will endure hardship as discipline, for God is treating me as His child. If I am not disciplined, then I am an illegitimate child and not a true child of God (Hebrews 12:8). And illegitimacy isn't for me. Therefore, I want to walk in my Father's truth even when it hurts and even when He's not telling me *why.* I know that what puzzles me now will "later on . . . produce a harvest of righteousness and peace" (Hebrews 12:11). For now, my discipline involves not knowing why.

True self-talk challenges every misbelieving attack on God's revelation of himself. It is an effort that requires diligence for a lifetime. But it can yield the firstfruits of peace and joy today.

Why not take time to pray and ask God to help you root out misbeliefs about Him?

Canoe Trip

YELLOW WATER LILY

(Or does it have another name?)
Opening its cup to disclose
   a tiny throne-room,
Shading from brilliant yellow
   to deep, deep red
      at the very centre
         around a golden throne.

They cast their crowns before the throne,
       singing,
"Worthy art thou, our Lord and God,
to receive glory and honour and power,
for thou didst create all things,
   and by thy will they existed
     and were created."

SEVEN

The Awful Thing

Have you ever wondered how it is that a certain couple can tragically lose a child and, though they grieve, their faith remains strong and steady? And how it is that another couple can also tragically lose a child and their lives are consumed with bitterness and hurt? How do some of us become fixated on demanding an answer to the unknowable?

We can also apply our questions to moral choices. How is it that one man would never consider concealing income when he reports what's taxable for the year? And how is it that another may claim all kinds of bogus deductions, saying, "When government does some shady things, why should I be honest?"

"Why?" is one of the most truly significant questions we can ask. It reveals the things that are most important to us, our sticking point, the line beyond which you and I will not go without a clear reason or answer.

In the last chapter, we considered that *knowing* why may not really be the highest good after all. But *asking* why is important. This is so because *it reveals to us the thing we have chosen as our own highest good*. Asking why is not simply a measure of faith or lack of faith, it actually reveals to us the person or thing in which our faith is invested. If this source does not come through for us in some way, we're left in pain, asking, "Why?"

Let me illustrate what I mean by relating a true account.

Theresa

Theresa came to our clinic after the collapse of another love affair sent her into an emotional tailspin. In her first visit, she said, "I want to find out why I always date guys who end up treating me like dirt!" She'd described the indecision and thoughtlessness of her recent boyfriend, Kris, his refusal to marry her, and his careless abusiveness.

"It's always like that," she'd insisted. "I seem to attract *that* kind the way a garbage truck attracts flies. That's me, the human garbage truck."

Of course I wanted to learn why she compared herself to a load of trash—why she'd come to believe she attracted only warped, undesirable, abusive males. In several sessions, we discovered that the groundwork for this conviction had been laid in the context of her first heterosexual relationship—the relationship with her father.

"After our last talk I remembered something that happened when I was real little," she said, beginning our eighth session. She was a lovely woman, whose soft brown eyes were growing misty as she spoke. "It happened when I was about four years old."

Theresa described the incident. Some twenty years before, on one particular Easter morning, she'd been thrilled with her new Easter outfit. Decked out in a frilly dress, hat, purse and small white gloves, she'd spun around before a full-length mirror, then run to show her daddy.

"I wanted so much for Daddy to think I was *pretty*," she said. "But he hardly looked at me. All he said was, 'Hurry up, or you'll be late for Sunday school.' " Tears were trailing down her cheeks.

She recalled numerous other incidents when she'd tried to capture her father's attention. The normal father instinctively signals in innumerable ways to his daughter that she is charming, attractive, feminine and important to him. Not Theresa's father. Despite her efforts, he remained cold and distant, at least as she saw it.

"*Nothing* worked," she said with frustration. "Once I even pulled his newspaper down and grinned at him over the top. He didn't even crack a smile. He said, 'Go and play.' I finally gave up trying."

Theresa had formulated a misbelief as a result of this neglect, and she still believed it: "Something is wrong with me, and there's nothing I can do about it. I don't have what it takes to interest him—or any other worthwhile man."

Consequently, she was involved with one ruinous man after another, and it wasn't because only losers were interested in her. Theresa routinely cold-shouldered intelligent and attractive men who might have appreciated and valued her. She felt comfortable with self-centered losers and uncomfortable with sensitive, strong males. Why? Because she believed any worthwhile man would see that she was not worth his time—that she was disposable. Trash.

As we talked, Theresa came to see that she held two false opinions. She realized that these misbeliefs were her problem, not some invisible rejection sticker or fatal curse. Wrong thinking led her to make wrong choices.

First, she was telling herself, "I can't be worth much if my own father never had time for me."

Second, even as a Christian, Theresa had never been able to believe God loved her. She labored under the idea that she could never prove herself good enough to deserve His love. To her, this string of terrible relationships "proved" God was not interested in blessing or helping her. She admitted, "I used to think God must hate me, otherwise He wouldn't have made my life so wretched. I guess I've always held it against Him for treating me so badly."

So there had been a rift with God, a separation from her only true and reliable Source of worth, love and acceptance. And in His place, Theresa had installed something that she considered to be the highest good. It's not even quite accurate to say that men became objects of her devotion. Her emotional energies were bent toward *being* someone's cherished companion. The object elevated above her altar was *self*. For at the bottom of it all, Theresa's self-talk told her: "Attention from a worthwhile man is the highest good." In short, she had made a false god of acceptance.

Conversely, rejection by men—and especially by men whom she thought of as the "bottom of the barrel"—was *the* most awful thing that could happen to her. From the very beginning, she'd had a rift with God, and she'd only widened it with her unbelief: "Sure God *says* He loves me, but that can't be true because He won't let me find the love I think I need."

What Makes You Think *That*?

For most people, overt rebellion against God is unthinkable. They're too scared of God to shake their fist at Him. Some aren't even aware that they're quarreling with Him. They got stuck, however, on a false good early in their development because of a difficult situation. How does this happen?

Earlier I defined the term misbelief, and have been using it throughout this text. Now it's vital to have an even deeper look at its theological origin and implications.

I found the term misbelief in the writings of Martin Luther, where it stands for wrong thinking prompted by the devil, the world, and the sinful human nature. Luther said it was men's wrong interpretation of events and their meanings that played a primary role in causing "despair" (bad feelings) and "vice" (bad behavior).

Recent research done by cognitive psychologists concurs with Luther's thoughts. Our bad feelings don't just fall on us out of the sky, nor do our undesirable choices and actions simply happen. It is the self-talk, what we tell ourselves inside, that causes emotions and behaviors.

If you stop and pay attention to your thoughts, you will discover yourself evaluating, reminding, propagandizing, assessing and interpreting the events of your everyday life. In short, we talk to ourselves all the time, actually telling ourselves what to think and feel about life's events. We usually do not respond *directly* to events themselves but to what we think about those events.

Here is where misbeliefs come in. Like Theresa, we all have some erroneous beliefs about reality. ("If my father doesn't love me, it means that no other male figure—including God—sees me as worthwhile.")

Life's experiences generate the wrong self-talk. ("Because this man treated me badly, it *proves* I'm unlovable.") The result is bad feelings (depression, loneliness, pain).

Hurt and loss, in turn, trigger anger. ("I didn't deserve that.") And, especially, anger at God. ("He's supposed to help, protect, prevent, provide—so why is He sleeping on the job?") And wrong conclusions about Him. ("He's powerless, uncaring—or else He doesn't exist.")

Thus, you can see that it isn't *events* that upset us but our misbeliefs about events and their meaning.

In trying to understand why circumstances are so difficult, then, children usually invent a theory or a hypothesis. These early childhood efforts to discover meaning in events usually result in wrong conclusions as to what is unthinkably bad (the awful thing) and the ideal solution to the problem (the highest good). These become radical (or *root*) misbeliefs that set their lives on a shaky foundation.[1]

Some children pick up their radical misbeliefs from simply hearing what their parents or other influential people say. "Strong women are bad." "Never marry a man who doesn't have a lot of money." These sentiments communicate that the most awful thing is to *be* or *be stuck with* a strong woman or a guy with only a meager income. Parental modeling and behavior can also convey these root

---

[1]For more on radical misbeliefs, see *Untwisting Twisted Relationships*, by Bill and Candy Backus, Bethany House Publishers.

attitudes, even if the words are never spoken.

Peers, too, can exert a powerful influence on beliefs and attitudes. So the fourteen-year-old whose friends proclaim that virginity is stupid may acquire the misbelief that the most awful thing in the world is to be a virgin.

After a little thought, you could probably finish the sentence: "The worst thing that could happen to me would be _____."

What would you put into the blank space? Poverty? Death? Torture? Nuclear war? Cancer? Alzheimer's disease? Loss of a child? Being rejected? What is the most awful thing that could happen to you? Maybe you have a list of "awful things" and can't quite decide which is worst.

In fact, *the* worst thing that can happen to any one of us is this: to become separated from God in our spirits, thoughts or actions. As long as you or I believe that something other than God is our highest good, we will remain subject to unhappiness and hopelessness.

I want to examine with you a few cases in which people were brought face-to-face with their own version of the most "awful thing." You'll see how they arrived at their false notion, why some remained unhappy, and how others became free.

Showing God How Good You Are

Chuck looked like anything but a chronic worrier, yet nervousness was destroying him. Sometimes this thirty-two-year-old guy, built like a linebacker for the Vikings, even made lists of bad things he could foresee happening.

Chuck was able to recall the point where he'd actually felt an inner rift opening up. At fourteen, he'd heard a hellfire evangelist preaching that the wages of sin is death. Fear motivated Chuck to hurry to the altar and accept Jesus Christ as his Savior and Lord. But soon after, he became aware of a problem.

Chuck could do nothing to please his dad. And when

Dad was displeased, life got miserable for the whole family, because he resorted to put-downs and angry silences that could keep everyone on edge for days. Chuck had taught himself how to carefully think ahead, surveying all the possible ways for things to go wrong and devising plans to avoid them. He came to believe it would be awful if anything should ever go wrong, because that would expose him to his dad's criticism, anger and habit of cutting people off emotionally.

And once he'd promised to obey God (who was even bigger and apparently more exacting than his father), the consequences of Chuck's sins and mistakes *had* to be much worse. Wasn't God supposed to be his heavenly *Father*? Maybe God was just a high-powered version of his earthly father, who was critical and demanding. Yes, he'd heard that we can humbly trust in Christ's love and righteousness, but Chuck's inner perception of reality—his family conditioning—told him otherwise.

Without knowing or intending it, Chuck disagreed with God's Word. He redoubled his own efforts, fearing that he could never be good enough for God to be pleased with him. He never saw that he was falling into the same kind of legalism that St. Paul warned the Galatians against, and he began to feel that the Christian life was a maze constructed by God to make him miserable. God was to be anticipated, dodged. God became an adversary.

Something else showed up in Chuck's psychological tests. He appeared so anxious to avoid criticism that he denied almost every item that might suggest problems. He tried so hard to appear fault-free that his Minnesota Multiphasic Personality Inventory (MMPI) proved invalid. His terrible fear of God's criticism was accompanied by a compulsion to avoid any criticism at all. He was becoming unrealistic and separated from the reality of his own flawed human nature. Denying his own weakness, he was actually becoming more susceptible to sin. For Chuck, the "awful thing" was to mess up and be subjected to criticism. Chuck believed:

> "If you're criticized, it means you've made an unforgivable mistake."

> "God won't let you get by with it, nor will anybody else. There is no forgiveness or restoration. You *have* to pay."

> "Making a mistake is the most *awful thing*. The *highest good* is to avoid any mistakes for the rest of your life. Sinless perfection."

You can see Chuck's rift with God over the good, a rift created by Chuck's radical misbelief, and amounting to a profound disagreement about the highest good. God would like to have opened Chuck's mind to the truth that:

1. Making a mistake is *not* the most awful thing; existing apart from Him is.
2. Avoiding all mistakes is *not* the highest good; God's forgiveness by grace is. The righteousness that's really worth having is Christ's unblemished righteousness. Chuck can have that as a gift if he will only accept it.

Can you see how Chuck's distress and compulsive perfectionism grew out of his rift with God over the good, his erroneous belief that God was wrong about the most awful thing?

Sadly, Chuck did not improve during our sessions together. He clung to his resolve to become perfect and absolutely beyond criticism. Even though he claimed to be a born-again Christian, he could not accept that we are "saved by grace through faith" and that it has nothing to do with our efforts but is a "gift of God—not by works, so that no one can boast" (Ephesians 2:8). He still relied on his list-keeping legalism and could not see that God's "works" are prepared by the Holy Spirit and that they are life-giving (see also v. 9, 10).

Ironically, Chuck's dialogue with God, if they'd come

face-to-face, might sound like this:

The Father: You're my son now because Jesus bought your righteousness with His blood. Now be at peace. Fellowship with me in prayer. I'm happy to tell you how to obey me, and I'll give you the power of my Spirit to help you and comfort you until you do it. I'm the author and finisher of your faith.

Chuck: Come on. No one's that good! There's got to be a catch. I know I'm supposed to rely on Jesus' finished work on the cross—but that doesn't sound right to me. I'm not taking any chances. I'm not going to trust in this kind, loving face you're putting on—only to get kicked in the teeth. No way!

Chuck's rift with God was still, unfortunately, as deep as ever when he left our counseling relationship.

While only some of us can identify with Chuck's perfectionism, almost everyone will recognize the pain of being criticized. And there's another tendency many of us share, spurred on by misbeliefs. It emerges in Ron's story.

Making Sure You'll Never Get Hurt

Ron, a bashful twenty-eight-year-old, with black hair and a beard like a storybook pirate, went through agony before he could explain why he'd come for help. With his eyes rivetted to the floor, he said, "I have a problem with masturbation. My church teaches it's wrong, and I feel guilty. I've tried to quit on my own, but I haven't been able to. I want to stop."

I gathered, from the tension in his voice and his distressed expression, that he was really suffering with this.

"Have you ever considered marriage?" I asked. "That's God's own arrangement for dealing with, among other things, your sexual needs." I hastened to add that it would be a mistake to marry someone merely to satisfy his drive for physical intimacy, but that one of the important purposes of marriage was to provide for our sexuality.

Ron's response was far more than I had expected. He spent most of an hour detailing how women had hurt him, disappointed him, failed to meet his expectations and so alienated him he'd nearly given up on women altogether. He recounted instance after instance in which girls he'd dated had taken advantage of him, let him down, or left him in the lurch. He went on to tell me about the sorry marital experiences of various friends, some pretty embittering stories.

Over a number of sessions, details of Ron's early years emerged.

Ron recalled an episode that perhaps laid the cornerstone for his misbeliefs, something that happened when he was about five. His mother had taken him along to her meeting at the local garden club and he'd been left to play with a little girl in a room while the ladies met in another. At the little girl's instigation, Ron crawled with her behind a sofa where they eventually began exploring each other's genitals. Curiosity rendered them oblivious to the approach of Ron's mother. When she saw what they were doing, she furiously yanked Ron from behind the sofa, turned him over her knee, and beat him publicly.

There were other episodes in which his mother had become enraged at him for similar "disgusting" actions that were, for the most part, normal childhood manifestations of sexuality.

Because of his mother's terrifying response to these experiments, Ron came to believe, not just that sex play was evil, but that his sexuality would disgust and anger women in general. Believing this, Ron had grown up expecting cruel treatment from girls. And so whenever he'd experienced the ordinary ups and downs of relationships his self-talk told him, "It's because they know what you're really thinking. You're disgusting."

Thus Ron's highest good was to stay "safe"—to avoid being hurt by a woman. His most "awful thing" was to be rejected or even to imagine he was rejected as a man. It was an attack on his maleness. This led him to believe he had to avoid any relationship that would mean vulnerability—*especially* marriage.

Some might find themselves agreeing with Ron's misbelief that the most awful thing is to be hurt. But does God agree? Helping Ron, in part, meant helping him to see how he'd fostered an unnecessary and painful rift with the God who taught us the importance of loving one another and proclaimed for all time that "it is not good for the man to be alone. Therefore I will make a helper suitable for him" (Genesis 2:18).

Ron did see how his misbeliefs had led him away from God's plan. Eventually, he began exploring relationships with the opposite sex. Though he was still a bachelor the last time I saw him, he has been forging ahead in his first trusting friendship with a woman. At last, he's able to be vulnerable, and to escape the lie that hurt is the very worst thing that can happen.

No Sense of Security

Mary Ellen had reached her sixty-fourth birthday, but memories of painful childhood deprivation were still vivid.

She'd been brought up during the Depression, the daughter of a dirt-poor farmer. There were times when the family had subsisted on beans for days at a time, living in shanties while her father picked up a few dollars here and there. To make it all worse, her mother habitually predicted the worst. Combined with the family's bleak economic straits, this produced in Mary Ellen a "habit" of insecurity.

To that day, Mary Ellen lived with the nagging torment that something bad was about to happen. She feared that she and her husband would lose everything they'd worked so hard for, despite the fact they were financially quite secure and were insured to the hilt.

For Mary Ellen, the most awful thing was to be without material necessities, and her highest good was to achieve a state in which there was no chance of suffering loss. Though she devoted most of her energies to the matter of security, she could never find herself secure enough to feel safe. Hence, her rift with God over "the awful thing" and the highest good.

According to Jesus, though, the highest good of all is the kingdom. We are to seek His kingdom first, not devote ourselves to accumulating money, which keeps us from being a good servant to our Lord and Master (Matthew 6:19–34). In God's eyes the good is to trade everything we own, if need be, to enter His kingdom—while the worst thing is never to find the doorway in.

Merton

For Merton, proving his masculinity was his first concern. Slight of build, kept home often from school because of various minor illnesses by his overprotective mother, and incompetent in team sports, Merton became the brunt of everybody's jokes. Kids even made fun of his name. Merton formulated the misbelief that he didn't have what it takes to be a real man, so he needed to act like a tough bully. When he did, the teasing stopped and others began to back off. "If I don't talk loud, act aggressive, and behave abrasively everywhere, people will doubt that I'm really a man; then they'll harm me," Merton told himself. Merton's awful thing was to be thought a sissy, less than a "real man." For him, the highest good was to convince everyone to the point where nobody would ever make fun of him or look down on him again. Tough masculinity became a false god.

Staying Thin

One group of sufferers known as anorexics and bulemics make themselves mortally ill by focusing their existence on becoming thin. Often, these are people who have, for various reasons, soaked up the notion that the ideal person is one who has no fat between skin and bones. Wan and curveless, their ideal image remains far removed from the distorted view they have of their own bodies as ugly, disgusting, and covered with rolls of revolting fat.

Sometimes these people have a history of abuse, psychological or sexual, in their childhoods. Growing up in an abusing, battering, chaotic world where even their bodies are subject to someone else's control, they theorize that the most awful thing is to have no control over your own person.[2] The media in a diet-and-exercise conscious culture suggest a means of control that nobody can take from them: weight control. Soon, control over weight marked by thinness becomes a way of life.

From movies, TV, fashion magazines and, perhaps, conversation with peers, these victims have formulated the radical misbelief that the most awful thing is to be fat, and being fat is the same as having any fat at all. A thin body, according to these people, is the greatest of all goods and that which is above all else worth living and (evidently for some with severe eating disorders) even dying for.

Home

During my own big rift with God, I believed that the highest good was my home and family. Since I was forced out of my home, deprived of my children and most of my income and property, I labeled all this intolerable. I firmly believed I could never recover from losing them.

I believe I came to my radical misbelief because of a

---

[2]This is not meant to oversimplify the complexities of eating disorders, only to place them in the context of this discussion.

catastrophic event in my early life: My family was shattered by the divorce of my parents. As a child, I decided nothing could be worse. I think most children of divorce resolve that, come what may, their own marriage must survive. But it is an error to tell yourself that the most awful thing is divorce. If you believe that, you are setting the stage for a potential rift with God and for untold wretchedness because of it. Even a thing so noble as a good home and family can become a substitute for God.

Major Misbeliefs About the Good

Study each of the following misbeliefs until you grasp how they all involve errors about the awful thing and its complement, the highest good. Each amounts to valuing something in the place of the only true highest good—God and His kingdom.

Your feelings are easily hurt. You may tell yourself, "It's imperative for me to get approval and positive feedback from everybody. If one person disapproves, I'll give up." The awful thing is human disapproval; the highest good is praise and appreciation.

You put off doing what you ought to do, or you fail to change bad behavior. You probably tell yourself, among other things, "I shouldn't have to do anything unpleasant, difficult, boring, or time-consuming to get what I want." The most awful thing is having to put up with unpleasantness, waiting or effort; the highest good is getting what you want easily.

"Other people cause my unhappiness," or, *"Circumstances make me upset."* Nearly everyone believes this one. The most awful thing is to have circumstances or people be less than perfect; the highest good is pleasant people and circumstances designed just for me.

You are depressed. Depressed persons almost always falsely devalue themselves with some variation on the theme, "I'm no good, worthless, incompetent, a failure." The awful thing is being me; the highest good is being someone else.

You worry a lot. You probably regale yourself with, "What if. . . ?" "What if x happens? Wouldn't it be horrible?" The awful thing is x; the highest good is insurance against x.

Or take the three misbeliefs routinely found in depressed people known as the "depressive triad": "I'm worthless; life for me is not worth living; the future is hopeless." In every one of them, the sufferer is devaluing something wrongly. Luke 15 presents, in graphic form, Jesus' revelation of the high value of even the most sinful person. First Corinthians 10:31 and Colossians 3:17 tell us that the most ordinary life, if lived to the glory of God, is valuable. And 1 Peter 1:3–5 tells us that God has created a living hope for us which remains in the future, however uncomfortable present circumstances may be.

The person who suffers from perfectionism holds the misbelief that a lesser good is the highest aim of life. Yes, it is good to be competent, adequate and achieving—but it's not essential that a person *always* be good in *everything.*

The anxious person's misbelief rests on the notion that the activity of thinking about disaster ahead of time will help stave off the disaster and that it's good to remind yourself over and over how awful things can be. In fact, imagining all possible disasters in the future is much better than letting God control your life and welcoming in childlike trust whatever He chooses to permit.

All the awful things and highest goods of our misbeliefs have a distinguishing feature: Not only are they erroneous, they are little, false religions. Each one proclaims that something other than God is ultimate. No wonder each one creates a rift with the true God.

It is God's way and His Word that defines the good, not mine or yours. Therefore, even things that occur contrary to our wishes can finally bring the highest possible good— if we allow God to shape us—because we are children of the Author of good and perfect gifts.

Finding Your Own False Beliefs

To help you get in touch with your own erroneous beliefs about the good, you might want to take a pencil and paper and try this exercise.

First, read the list that follows and note the beliefs you can identify with. These are clues to your own emotional or behavioral difficulties. They don't necessarily mean you are mentally ill, merely that certain feelings or actions give you some difficulty.

Second, translate each misbelief into a statement about your awful thing or highest good. ("People should love me" translates: "It's an awful thing when everybody isn't giving me approval and affection," and "the highest good is to bask in attention and admiration.")

Third, try to frame your own statements of disagreement with God about the good. ("Why do you allow *her* to get all the attention and admiration, God, when I'm more deserving?")

Fourth, analyze your misbeliefs to discover in what way they amount to mental idolatry. In this way, you will see your own rift with God.

Here's the list (and don't forget to think through others that apply to you):

＿＿ People should love me.
＿＿ People should approve of me.
＿＿ People should understand me.
＿＿ I have to be perfect.
＿＿ I have to be the best.
＿＿ I have to be right.
＿＿ I shouldn't have to do difficult, unpleasant

work to change. It should be easy for me.

_____ If something doesn't go the way I want it to, I'll be upset.

_____ When people don't pay attention to me, I can't be happy.

_____ People must live up to my expectations, or I will be miserable.

_____ When my spouse doesn't consider my feelings, he/she is awful. It's terrible to be married to such a person.

_____ I should be able to get my way and be happy by sitting back and waiting until others do what I like.

The Rift Is Not God's Idea

You shall have no other gods before me. You shall not make for yourself an idol in the form of anything in heaven above or on the earth beneath or in the waters below. You shall not bow down to them or worship them; for I, the Lord your God, am a jealous God. (Exodus 20:3)

God doesn't hate idolatry because He's an egotist, but because people who fill their minds with untruth open a rift between themselves and the truth. In so doing, they cannot help but cause their own downfall.

Solomon tells us that the fear of the Lord (not the idolatrous fear of what others think, nor the fear of loss, nor the fear of injury, nor the fear of any other most awful thing) is the starting point of wisdom. And wisdom is to turn from idolatry toward God. Telling yourself the truth, that is, reconciling yourself with the God of truth, will lead to the rewarding life promised in Scripture (see Proverbs 1:1–7).

Consider what wisdom will do for you:

For the Lord gives wisdom, and from his mouth

come knowledge and understanding. He holds victory in store for the upright, he is a shield to those whose walk is blameless, for he guards the course of the just and protects the way of his faithful ones. Then you will understand what is right and just and fair—every good path. For wisdom will enter your heart [the place of internal monologue], and knowledge will be pleasant to your soul. (Proverbs 2:6–13)

The Lord is the everlasting God, the Creator of the ends of the earth. He will not grow tired and weary, and his understanding no one can fathom. He gives strength to the weary and increases the power of the weak. Even youths grow tired and weary, and young men stumble and fall; but those who hope in the Lord will renew their strength. They will soar on wings like eagles; they will run and not grow weary, they will walk and not be faint. (Isaiah 40:28–31)

As you reread these scriptures, contrast the vivid descriptions of God's boundless superiority with your own false "ultimates." What Isaiah wants you to understand is that by getting the truth about God into your self-talk, you will live the "life on wings" he described, instead of living the hopeless, defeated, harassed existence that idols or false ultimates deliver.

And consider this sobering passage as a warning from a loving Father who does not want you to suffer:

The wrath of God is being revealed from heaven against all the godlessness. . . . God's invisible qualities—his eternal power and divine nature—have been clearly seen, being understood from what has been made, so that men are without excuse. For although they knew God, they neither glorified him as God nor gave thanks to him, but their thinking became futile and their foolish hearts were darkened. . . . They exchanged the truth of God for a lie, and worshiped and served created things rather than the Creator—who is forever praised. (Romans 1:18, 20)

If you have a rift with God over any false idol, then to that extent you have exchanged the truth of God for a lie. So the pain in your life and relationships may be the wrath of God revealed from heaven. He cannot bless and approve an action or belief that removes us, His children, from our Source of life and well-being. You can find biblical instructions for healing that rift, not only here, but also by reading the entire Epistle to the Romans. There, God reveals the way to peace and reconciliation with himself.

There is another option, of course. You can press on, insisting that God come to the fore, stand with His toes on the line, and give an accounting.

It's time to have a look at where our demands leave us when we refuse to find rest in His Word.

Canoe Trip

CLOUD-ROCKS

Under the surface of the water,
Seemingly so solid,
    immovable.
We touch them with our paddles,
    hesitantly,
Finding them to be
    mere clouds;
Strange, underwater clouds,
Dim shadows of reality.

For now we see in a mirror dimly,
    but then face to face
Now I know in part;
    then I shall understand fully,
Even as I have been fully understood.

EIGHT

Where the Rift Leaves You

When I considered telling the story of my own rift with God, which appears in the first chapter, I was concerned. Would some readers be so shocked and offended by my anger at God that they'd close the book and not read another word?

Because I've listened to so many friends and clients struggle to be honest about their feelings, I believe that those who have always experienced perfect peace with God are a very small group indeed.

Most believers I know have felt shock and hurt at what appears to be God's "shabby" treatment of them.

"God discriminates against me," one woman complained. To her, it was God's fault that she was still unmarried. "Other people get what they ask for. But when *I* pray for what I want, He gives me the opposite. I used to have a boyfriend—but since I've been praying for a husband, I don't even get dates anymore."

Ivan, Dostoyesvsky's atheist, whom we read about in Chapter Three, was more than offended, hurt or shocked. He had done away with God altogether. He had committed, at least in his own mind, *deicide*. He had killed off God.

Of course there are many, even "believing" Christians, who have not done away with God, but have effectively thrown away their faith in Him. I wonder sometimes if believers are not more susceptible to spiritual wounding because they believe in Him so passionately and expect so fervently that He will do what they ask. One writer has

discussed the effects of this wounding in a book called
Disappointment With God.[1]

Call these emotions what you will—disappointment,
hurt, anger, bitterness. One basic fact remains: You can't
have hostile feelings toward God, however buried they may
be, without bearing the consequences in your own person
and in your relationships with others. The rift with God
is a corrosive ingredient in the spiritual and emotional
stew. And undealt with, it brings far-reaching consequences.

A "Loose Cannon" in the Universe

*The rift leaves you wandering alone in an imper-
sonal universe, where God is only a blind force who neither notices nor cares.* Recently, I heard an address by a
theologian who had nearly been killed by a brutal assail-
ant. After a long period of convalescence, her wounds had
healed so that she could again enter the pulpit, and she
spoke for the first time publicly about her catastrophe.
Though it was very difficult for her, she maintained gracious dignity while describing the horrors she'd experienced.

What caught my attention most was how she perceived
God's role. She denied that God had caused her adversity;
she denied that He had willed it; she denied that He had
permitted it. In short, she told us He had nothing whatever to do with it. As I pondered her message, I realized
that her way to handle her tragedy was *not* to turn to the
God of the Bible, but to strain doctrine and logic. To her,
God was no longer the One who knows and cares when a
single sparrow falls to the ground. In effect, she *very
nearly* killed off God.

Many like her distill their anger into concentrated denial of God's involvement in their lives. Some erect a phil-

[1]Yancey, Phillip, *Disappointment With God: Three Questions No One Asks
Aloud* (Grand Rapids, Mich.: Zondervan, 1988.)

osophical framework, maintaining that He initiated the universe, hammered some laws into it, set it in motion and then retired to a state of eternal inactivity, leaving creation to run all by itself for an allotted time. In short, they emasculate the Almighty.

When we claim that man's free will is greater than Divine intervention, we pay a heavy price. How can you or I offer any meaningful prayer to a God who is less than we are? Or less than He himself claims to be?

If, by allowing your rift with God to grow, you deny Him a significant place in your history, you must face this alarming reality: If He is not there or does not care about you, you are terribly, helplessly small and alone in a huge universe.

The rift leaves you in complete command of your life. You are your own god. This one might sound appealing at first. ("Great! I get to run my own life!") Many are thrilled to think they have the power and the right to choose for themselves. In reality, though, it is a terrible state of affairs when God finally does brush off His hands and say, "Choose your own way and do whatever you like. I'm through with you!"

In Romans, Paul defines the wrath of God as the state in which God has given up with a person. He steps back to let you become completely responsible. Then there is no one to turn to who really knows for sure. No one to rely on who has all the power to do what needs to be done. There is only little you, doing your own thing.

The rift leaves you in rebellion. A small example of this once occurred in our family. I want to tell you about it to illustrate how quickly anger, even over trivialities, can turn into a rift—and an attempt to "unseat" God from His throne.

Once the Backus family owned two horses, Shadrach and Meshach (we never managed to find a suitable Abednego). They were the apple of my wife's eye. Candy loved those animals devotedly.

We boarded them on a nearby farm, and one day the horses escaped. If they chose to do so, they could have explored the entire upper Midwest.

A day went by. Then two days. The horses were nowhere to be found. Candy became more and more distraught. By the second night, she was certain her horses had been stolen and that she'd never see them again. She cried, and nothing could console her.

Then she became resentful. I was quite amazed to hear her say, "God can't possibly mean what He says in His Word. How can He let this happen? What's the use of going to church and praying?" As she saw it God had not done His job. And her response was anger, which was turning into rebellion.

Today, Candy looks back on this episode with chagrin. We both smile when we think of the tender, fatherly love that tolerated and gently corrected this rebellious outburst. (Incidentally, we found the horses contentedly munching on a neighbor's hay.)

I wonder how many times a day God is the target of someone's rebellion over small things that go wrong— things that are often due more to our own carelessness than to a failure to protect and provide on His part.

The rift can make you determined to "show" God! Mickey slammed the car door, stalked into the tavern and bellied up to the bar. He ordered a double martini, extra dry. He was determined to get drunk because "God had it coming."

Even after all his hard work, his sacrifice, prayer, reading the Bible and a struggle to stay dry, God hadn't shown him any signs of love. Mickey had prayed for a promotion. Ken got it instead, even though his qualifications were weak. And, besides, Mickey had *prayed.*

Downing his first martini, he thought, *I was so stupid*

*to believe all that trash about God's promises. I'm
through trying to please Him. I'm going to quit this stinking company.* He'd show God that he could be a success
without any so-called help from Him.

That's the way it is for so many who become angry at
God: They set out to "make God sorry" that He failed them
so miserably. They redouble their efforts and even achieve
great things, among other things, to prove that they can
get along fine without God's help. They expect, but usually
do not get, satisfaction out of doing whatever they can to
pay God back.

*The angry rift leaves you cut off from the Source of
life, power, love and answered prayer.* As you drift further from Him on an undercurrent of anger, something
recedes from your grasp—that is, the resources a human
being must have to remain spiritually alive. You find it
harder to pray and you have less expectation that God will
answer. The inner empowerment for living will slowly fade,
because life comes from the Holy Spirit when a believer is
in fellowship with God. If you shove the Spirit out of your
heart, *death* is the biblical name for your condition.
Though your heart hasn't stopped beating yet, you are
spiritually dying.

Michael, I think, was experiencing this kind of death.

Michael

Michael, a sixty-two-year-old client, had been depressed since the death of his wife three years before. He
folded his hands in his lap and leaned toward me to explain the reason for his visit. I'll try to record our conversation for you:

Michael: Nothing has been the same. I ought to snap out
of it, but—well, why did Betty have to leave me
just when we were going to enjoy life? We'd paid
our mortgage. The last kid had moved out. I was

going to retire early so we could travel. Then she got cancer and died.

Backus: You talked about Betty "leaving you." Is that how you think of her death?

Michael: I guess it is. I feel as if she's gone and left me all alone. I know in my head Betty couldn't help getting sick. But I wonder—*why?* What kind of God would let that awful cancer take my wife just when everything was going to be good for us?

Backus: Are you saying it's hard to understand how such a God could be called a God of love and compassion?

Michael: That's right. How could He be so cruel? That's what bothers me so much.

Backus: What is it you're feeling?

Michael: I haven't *let* myself think about it much, but underneath I have had some bad feelings toward God. I haven't felt like praying. I still go to church sometimes, but it seems dead. Or maybe I feel dead. Maybe both. I suppose I do hold it against God that He took Betty away. I guess I just can't see how He could do it to me. And I'm not too happy with Him for it. Maybe I've drifted away from Him.

For a number of sessions Michael struggled to get in touch with his unexamined feelings of resentment toward God. He found that much of the misery he'd attributed to loss was really bitterness directed toward God, who "could have healed Betty's cancer." The irony was that Michael's spiritual health was being eaten away by the cancer of anger, producing the depression for which he had consulted me.

When anger pushes God out of a person's heart, the effect on one's emotional life is devastating. A psychologist may fail to see it, however, because of a common preconception that spiritual issues only represent neurotic conflicts. This causes many therapists to remain blind to the deeper reality of this happening within someone's soul. A person *can* be angry with God, and it is not helpful to hide this fact by theorizing that he's really angry at his father.

Anger with God can drive you to harmful behaviors that will only ruin you. Let me tell you briefly about Jon, a young man who used illicit sex to "fight" God.

You would never have dreamed what was beneath Jon's passive exterior and the fixed angelic smile. He was twenty-nine, with blond, wavy hair and blue eyes, and it seemed incredible that he could be anything but a first-place winner in the arena of love.

But Jon was no winner. True, his good looks made sexual conquest easy. Without a hint of exaggeration, he told me he'd gone to bed with maybe a hundred women or more. He said this practice, which he'd come to hate, was all he could do because he was so starved for love and closeness. "Why doesn't God give me someone to really love me?" he asked during an early visit.

Finally, Jon began asking himself what he was really getting out of his promiscuous bedding of women since it had long since ceased to be fun. He realized he felt driven. But by what?

"You know," he mused in my office one day, "I kind of enjoy the idea that God doesn't like what I'm doing."

"How do you mean?" I posed.

"Well, I get ticked off at God when every woman I date for a while turns out wrong. Sometimes I even notice myself thinking, 'I'll get Him. I'll just go pollute myself, kind of wallow in filth.' I know it's bad for me and that's exactly why I want to do it. Do you understand?"

I was beginning to. It appeared that deep down he had blamed each failure on his heavenly Father. He was acting out his anger by turning on *himself,* trying to clobber God by demolishing his own sexuality and humanity.

Anger with God leaves you willing to harm others. Occasionally, people present themselves for treatment, saying they don't want to be there. That was the case with Rhoda. But she had no choice, she said, because she'd been ordered by a judge to get treatment.

Rhoda was a single parent with one child, Jeannie, a ten-year-old whom she'd been abusing. Now the girl had been removed from home, to be returned only after Rhoda completed treatment.

Reluctant though she was, she finally admitted to attacking her daughter with a pair of scissors. "But I didn't intend to stab or cut her. I just hit her with them. The points *accidentally* cut her on the side of the neck. She told someone at school how she got cut, and one of the teachers reported it to Child Protection."

Gradually, I learned Rhoda had used the scissors in this way before. Yes, Jeannie had accidentally gotten cut and, yes, she had hit Jeannie with other things—a coat hanger, a stick, a knife. But nobody had reported her before. She felt bad, she said, and wanted her daughter back. That was the only reason she was coming to see me. She really didn't want to lose Jeannie.

"But she pesters me day and night without a break. I've got to punish her some way. It gets so bad, I see red. Then I lash out. Okay, so I've injured her. I know I'm a terrible mother. A bad person. Isn't that what you want to hear?"

Rhoda herself had been abused. Her mother regularly beat her until she was bruised and had to wear long dresses and long sleeves to school to hide her injuries. But she had survived.

When I asked about her relationship with God, she shot back, "I hate Him! He never did anything for me! Where was He when my mother was smacking *me* around? Where was He when Roger got me pregnant and then pulled out of my life after promising me the moon? Where was God when I was in that hospital delivering Jeannie all by myself? Where was God when I cried and begged for help for my baby? God is a failure as far as I'm concerned. He doesn't care about me, and I don't have any use for Him!"

"Do you think God doesn't care if you harm Jeannie?"

"If He does care, if it bothers Him, then I say *good*. He's got it coming!"

Yes, in some people the angry rift pushes toward vicious attacks on other people, even on those they love.

Axioms From the Angry Rift

The angry rift with God is based on colossal misbeliefs. Chief among them (as we've seen earlier): *God is wrong about what is good for me.* But the angry person does emphasize some *truths*, too:

God is in charge. Some well-meaning people point out to their afflicted friends that the evil isn't God's doing. He does only the good. But the Bible occasionally says evil events are sent directly from God (see 1 Samuel 16:14–16ff.; 2 Samuel 12:11; 2 Chronicles 34:24). More often we are told that Satan originates our disasters. Nevertheless, we can't forget that God *is* in charge. Though He could stop evil, He sometimes does not. No amount or type of evil can prove that God is *not* in charge.

God can and does rein-in the devil. Though He does occasionally permit evil to work some awful things in human lives, He always sets limits. Satan cannot pass those limits. We can legitimately infer from the scene of the heavenly throne room shown us in the first chapter of Job that God holds Satan like a big dog on a leash, so he can only go so far and no further.

God knows, better than we know, how to turn the effects of evil into good. He says:

For my thoughts are not your thoughts, neither are your ways my ways. . . . As the heavens are higher than the earth, so are my ways higher than your ways and my thoughts than your thoughts. . . . You will go out in joy and be led forth in peace; the mountains and hills will burst into song before you, and all the trees of the field will clap their hands. Instead of the thornbush will grow the pine tree, and instead of briers the myrtle will grow. (Isaiah 55:8–13)

The thornbush and the briers were permitted by God, but He has a plan to turn things around so the fragrant pine tree and the lovely myrtle spring up in their place.

You cannot escape God. He is in charge. His will for you is good. Your rift with Him won't change the reality that He exists. You cannot dissolve Him into nothingness. If this is so, and if there is evil in the world and in our lives, we'd better take a good look at the truth about God. Who is He?

Considering the number of popular and laundered theologies about who God is, I believe we need to take a careful look at what *God* says about himself.

Tired

Somehow I will continue to work
  amid the tasks of autumn,
    still gathering,
      preserving,
      giving shelter;
    longing still to hear,
"Well done, you good and faithful servant,"
    but faltering now
    and wanting more
    to know the sleep
      of winter.

  But I have promises to keep,
  and miles to go
  before I sleep.

The Lord God has given me
the tongue of those who are taught,
that I may know how to sustain with a
word
  him that is weary.
Morning by morning he wakens,
  he wakens my ear
to hear as those who are taught.
The Lord has opened my ear,
and I was not rebellious,
I turned not backward.

NINE

Who Does God Think He Is?

During the time when I believed my world was shattered, I *thought* I knew the truth about God. But I only knew one sense of the word.

I knew the Catechism's right answers about God and His attributes. But the whole time I *told myself* something else. I stored truth on shelves somewhere in the back of my brain, while I actively applied wrong beliefs to my life. This "split-mind" condition led to trouble and instability, just as the Epistle of James warns that it will (see James 1:6–8).

The amazing, and *sad* thing is that when you are double-minded you don't see your true condition. You are lost in a mental, spiritual fog. You accept contradictions because you think religious "truth" is lovely-sounding, even if it doesn't work in practice.

For example, you might "know" that God is love (1 John 4:8), but tell yourself, "He doesn't care about me at all because He allowed _____ to happen." But a God who loves cannot also be uncaring.

The beliefs by which I was operating after my divorce were totally opposite from the truths in the back of my brain. Here, as accurately as I can now recall them, are some of the rotting planks of self-talk beneath my painful everyday life:

"The life which was my first choice is gone, so I'm left with broken pieces. I have to endure misery from now on. My life is mostly over and everything important is gone."

"I'm going to be all alone in the world because nobody loves me, and nobody ever will. Something must be terribly wrong with me. I'm such a loser, I'd better not get married again."

"God is no help. Religion is a waste of time. Christianity is irrelevant to life. To me, psychology offers more profound understanding. The real answer must lie in knowing the operation of the mind. Surely what *I* need is to be found in mastering the science of personality."

"Since I've been treated badly, I have a right to indulge myself, to let my desires have free rein—it will make up for some of what I've lost! I think I owe myself a little misbehavior. Look where being good got me."

"I'm going to join the crowd. The world is full of people having fun: drinking, smoking, rocking to music. I'm sick and tired of trying to keep all the tiresome, legalistic commandments—they're probably out-of-date anyway."

Do you tell yourself distortions about who God is? Tune in to your own self-talk as it passes through your mind when you're unhappy with your circumstances:

"God doesn't love me—not really—because I'm not lovable."

"God is obviously out to *get* me!"

"God doesn't care about me as much as He cares about the 'saints,' the holy types, the talented, the good-looking, the smooth-talkers, the brilliant, shiny, squeaky clean, the unblemished."

"If only I could get God to answer my prayers, then I'd know He truly loves me."

"I can't trust God not to hurt me."

"What God has let happen to me shouldn't happen!"

"He is wrong, unfair, unjust!"

"I know better than God about what's good for me."

Because these misbeliefs attack God's character, they are powerful and they can work enormous harm. Their power springs from what you are experiencing at the moment, instead of from the Word of God, which abides forever (see Isaiah 40:38). Beliefs based *solely* on experience lead to wrong conclusions about the nature of God. And because of that, they are dangerous.

When I finally opened myself to God—over and above and *instead* of my beliefs about Him—I suddenly came to know Truth in a different, revolutionary way. Truth was a standard by which to judge my experience. This was the opposite of what I'd been doing. I no longer had to be thrown and bruised by circumstances. I could be strong in my inner man because I could stop tormenting myself with lies, and begin building myself up with the truth.

What *is* the truth about God? What do you need to store in your truth library, so that you can combat your own misbelieving internal monologue?

The One True God

Here are some of the things God says about himself:

God is the One who loves you nonstop. "I have loved you with an everlasting love; I have drawn you with lovingkindness" (Jeremiah 31:3).

God loves you even when you don't love or serve Him—even when you're sinning. "But God demonstrates his own love for us in this: While we were still sinners, Christ died for us" (Romans 5:8).

God is for you, not against you; your Ally, not your Enemy; your Helper, not your Destroyer. "If God is for us, who can be against us? He who did not spare his own Son, but gave him up for us all—how will he not also, along with him, graciously give us all things?" (Romans 8:31, 32).

God has specific plans for us. What He plans for us is good, not bad. " 'For I know the plans I have for you,' declares the Lord, 'plans to prosper you and not to harm you, plans to give you hope and a future. Then you will call upon me and come and pray to me, and I will listen to you. You will seek me and find me when you seek me with all your heart. I will be found by you' " (Jeremiah 29:11–14).

God always does right by us; He never does wrong by us. "O God, . . . your right hand is filled with righteousness" (Psalm 48:10).

God's deeds in our lives are right, fair, and just—never wrong, never mistaken, never unfair or unjust. "You answer me with awesome deeds of righteousness, O God our Savior, the hope of all the ends of the earth" (Psalm 65:5).

Clearly, God's view of himself, as set forth in the Word, conflicts with the assertions of our rift-creating misbeliefs. Let's be even more specific.

When *We* Say . . . God Says . . .

When we say, "God made me lose my job," or "made my child ill," or "made me marry a loser," or "made me fail in business"—God answers that He does only good, not evil:

> Taste and see that the Lord is good; blessed is the man who takes refuge in him. (Psalm 34:8)
> The Lord our God is righteous in everything he does. (Daniel 9:14)
> The Lord is upright; he is my Rock, and there is no wickedness in him. (Psalm 92:15)

When we say, "Maybe God loves some people, but He doesn't love me"—God says He loves *you* specifically, even if you have become separated from Him by a rift:

The Son of Man came to seek and to save what was lost. (Luke 19:10)

Jesus answered them, "It is not the healthy who need a doctor, but the sick. I have not come to call the righteous, but sinners to repentance." (Luke 5:31, 32)

God so loved *the world* that He gave His only Son. (John 3:16)

When we say, "God has forgotten me"—God says He can't forget you because He keeps you in His own self-talk. Furthermore, He never stops talking to himself about you!

Zion said, "The Lord has forsaken me, the Lord has forgotten me." But I say, "Can a mother forget the baby at her breast. . . ? Though she may forget, I will not forget you! See, I have engraved you on the palms of my hands." (Isaiah 49:14–16)

When we say, "God doesn't answer my prayers"—He says He *will* answer them. When the time is exactly right. And that time will be soon, even if it seems like a long delay. (Just hang in there!):

Before they call I will answer; while they are still speaking I will hear. (Isaiah 65:24)

And Jesus told His disciples . . . that they should always pray and not give up. "And will not God bring about justice for his chosen ones, who cry out to him day and night? Will he keep putting them off? I tell you, he will see that they get justice, and quickly." (Luke 18:1–8)

When we say, "God doesn't keep His word or fulfill His promises to me"—He says He never lies and can't break a promise:

God did this [took an oath, swearing to Abraham that He would perform His promise] so that, by two unchangeable things in which it is impossible for God to lie, we who have fled to take hold of the hope offered to us may be greatly encouraged. We have this hope as an anchor for the soul, firm and secure. (Hebrews 6:18, 19)

When we say, "God is unfair and unjust, and the circumstances He has handed to me are terrible"—God says He is never unfair or unjust. He also says we are in no position to pass judgment on Him. He knows much that we don't know. So if we think we're right and He's wrong, it is our belief that must change:

> Who is this that darkens my counsel with words without knowledge? Brace yourself like a man; I will question you, and you shall answer me. Where were you when I laid the earth's foundation? Tell me, if you have understanding. (Job 38:2–4)

When we say, "I know God's commandments direct me to do so-and-so, but I have this need that must be fulfilled, so just this once I have to believe it's good for me to do what He has forbidden (or not to do what He has commanded)"—God says He knows more than we do. He wills our good, and His commandments order us to do *only* what is *good* for us, whether we see it or not:

> Keep [God's] decrees and commands, which I am giving you today, so that it may go well with you and your children after you and that you may live long in the land the Lord your God gives you." (Deuteronomy 4:40)
>
> If you pay attention to the commands of the Lord your God that I give you this day and carefully follow them, you will always be at the top, never at the bottom. (Deuteronomy 28:13)

The Difference Between *What* and *How*

While I was a very young seminarian, taking wonderfully enlightening classes on theology, I crafted what I thought was the sermon to end all sermons. It was on gratitude. I covered the subject; I left nothing out. It came back from the professor approved for preaching!

With deep satisfaction, I preached it to a little congregation in Illinois. Afterward, I stood at the door, shaking hands with the farmers and their families who made up the parish. Only one man frowned at me and said, "You told us plenty about *what* to do. But you didn't tell us *how*."

This was not exactly the sort of comment I'd hoped for. It hit me in the solar plexus. I couldn't quit thinking about it. Late that night, still nursing my wounded ego, I pored over it again. The man was right: It was full of good material on what true gratitude is; but I hadn't even touched on how an ungrateful person can become grateful.

Since then I've listened to a heap of sermons—some of them great. And I've heard some that were not so hot. Often, even the good ones failed to pass the "Frowning Illinois Farmer Test." They had plenty on *what* but little or nothing on *how*.

That, of course, is the big question: How do you go about getting yourself to agree with God—when everything inside you wants to disagree? How do you get those scriptural beliefs off the dusty shelf in the back of your mind and watch them become "living and active and sharper than any two-edged sword"? (Hebrews 4:12).

In the next chapter, we will consider how we can turn the situation around—how we begin to heal the rift with God.

Canoe Trip

CAMEL LAKE

Hungry and tired,
　　close of the day;
Far end of the lake,
　　and no place to stay.
Only a long portage ahead,
　　and not a campsite to be seen.
Four anxious children,
　　we paddle in our separate ways,
Two canoes, combing the shoreline
　　once again.

Then comes the shout,
　　"We found one!"
How could we have missed it?
Long, flat rock,
　　level ground for tents,
　　　　plenty of firewood;
　　　　　　and we give thanks.

Therefore do not be anxious . . .
　　for your heavenly father knows
　　　　that you need them all.

TEN

Agreeing With God

Lorna had lost her usual effervescence when our counseling together uncovered painful feelings. Once we got beneath the surface, her very private wounds showed: Though she was married to a prominent and well-liked politician, Lorna felt she had "zero" importance.

As we talked, I heard how Lorna had learned to fade into the woodwork, except on those occasions when she had to stand beside her husband on a platform or submit to interviews for women's magazines (which usually focused on what she fed him for breakfast). As a result, Lorna's lifelong misbelief that she was inferior had etched itself deeper. And now that her husband was required to travel on political business she was left alone, feeling unwanted and useless.

Gradually, as we worked together, she'd arrived at a truer self-assessment. For instance, she had led some twenty-eight people to Christ. I'd asked her, then, to search the Bible for what God had to say about her personal significance and her service in His kingdom. She'd returned with a good list. ("There is joy in heaven over one sinner who repents" . . . "The Father himself loves you" . . . and more.) Lorna had no trouble articulating the appropriate conclusions: She was a worthwhile person; she had meaning, both for her valuable work done for Christ and her intrinsic worth to God.

I suggested she get a job or do volunteer work to make the most of the hours Pete's absence made available to her. Even more important, I recommended that she use her understanding of the truth to replace her misbeliefs.

It was then Lorna responded, "I know *intellectually* that all you say is right. But I still *feel* bad."

I wish I had a dollar for every time someone has made that statement to me. For many, it's not that difficult to learn what the truth is—especially if they're Christians, with a knowledge of the Bible. But it's sometimes hard to root out and *change* the misbeliefs in our belief systems even when we "know" better.

Why Is Change So Hard?

Change is never as easy as maintaining the status quo. Why? For one thing, practicing a behavior again and again wears deep grooves in your mind, so to speak, which turn into ruts. So it's hard to quit smoking, give up coffee, or stop passing around juicy gossip when you've been doing such things for years. Physical habits can be difficult to release, and so are habitual beliefs and self-talk.

Second, you and I often get some reward from our misbeliefs.

For instance, let's say you're a person who constantly expresses low self-esteem. ("I'm so dumb. No one could ever like me.") Maybe others have responded with reassurance. ("Oh no! You're a wonderful person!") Or maybe they've worked extra hard to keep you happy.

I remember a bookkeeper who told himself he was too anxious to write without shaking. And it was true. His writing was so bad he couldn't do his work. He went on unemployment compensation, but that ran out. Then he was declared disabled by a psychiatrist, so he received aid for the disabled. When I saw him for treatment, it was impossible to change his anxiety-arousing misbeliefs. He was getting paid for keeping them! That kind of reward for a misbelief practically insures you won't change.

Sometimes, a misbelief is hard to change because we organize our lives around it. For example, Jerry told himself from the time he was a teenager, "My life will have meaning only if people listen to my opinions and give me their attention and praise." Motivated by this misbelief, rather than a genuine call from God, Jerry entered the parish ministry knowing that he could surround himself with people who would give him their constant approval and attention. For Jerry, changing his outrageous ego problem required leaving the ministry. Because he'd fashioned his life to feed his internal falsehoods, he couldn't replace his misbeliefs with the truth: He really didn't need everyone's attention all the time!

Like Jerry, others who have built their lives around a misbelief usually have to make major changes in order to get well. And that requires a big decision.

You and I may have trouble changing a misbelief because it gives us license to hurt someone with whom we're furious. ("She's got it coming!") Or to take something that isn't ours. ("He owes it to me!") Or to do something forbidden. ("I owe it to myself.") In short, some people have invested everything in a misbelief.

If your misbeliefs are tenacious, then be honest about what's motivating you to hang on to it and have the courage to change—whatever it may take.

We Need the Spirit of Truth

There is only One in all the universe who can truly help us to exchange misbeliefs for the truth: He is the Holy Spirit of truth. I believe it's impossible to make yourself agree with God from the heart without His Spirit's deep work in your life. Here is how you make the simple, first steps if you have never done so.

You begin by confessing to God that you want and need Him. You acknowledge that His Son, Jesus, is your Savior—the only one who can save you from sin and death. If you haven't opened your heart to Jesus Christ, if you haven't accepted Him as your only hope for forgiveness, renewal and salvation, you can do that now. Jesus pledges that God will send the Holy Spirit to dwell in you. And He will enable you to agree with God. He will give you a heart-grip on the truth that will make it real and alive.

The "condition" that the Holy Spirit brings to you is called *faith*. It's the ability to believe; it's like the chemical that added to a storage battery makes it capable of receiving an electrical charge. This comes from God as a gift. When Jesus promised to send the Holy Spirit as Counselor to His disciples, He specifically pledged that the Spirit would "remind" them of the truth He had previously spoken (John 14:26). They already knew the words and, for the most part, had consented that what Jesus said was correct. But they needed to have words of truth explode with such power inside them that "reality" changed. Isn't that what you've been hoping for?[1]

The Holy Spirit works by means of God's Word. Practically speaking, this means that you and I must prayerfully ponder the Word of God, asking Him to make its truth alive by the power of the Spirit. That is the beginning, the point at which we open the door to the Spirit of truth.

You Do the Believing

As we've noted, faith is a gift from God. But Paul describes His Word as a sword that you and I must wield (Ephesians 6:17). You and I must energetically, resolutely, firmly, even mulishly *insist* that the old, God-hating misbeliefs have to go, and we must daily practice telling ourselves the truth. This means deliberately silencing our misbeliefs at the moment they're voiced within, "thrusting through" these lies, as it were, with God's word of truth. This is our part in the spiritual battle (see Ephesians 6:12).

To continually win these daily skirmishes, you and I must learn to *do* a number of things. For having faith is

---

[1]For a Scripture study on the Holy Spirit's ability to plant the truth in your heart, see 1 Corinthians 2:13, 14 and Ephesians 2:8, 9.

anything but passive and quiet. We can get to work with the following plan:

Pay attention to your self-talk. "Know yourself," said Socrates. If you practice you can develop constant awareness of the beliefs and misbeliefs running through your head at any given moment. When you feel bad, irritable, depressed, upset—stop and listen to what you are thinking or telling yourself. *Tune in.*

Seek the truth all the time. When you're tempted to ignore or override the truth, be ruthless. Ask: "What am I telling myself *now*?" If you don't see why your damaging self-talk is false or erroneous, get busy. Ask others. Check your logic. Above all, go to the Bible if the subject you're questioning is taught there. Don't rest until you're sure you've found the flaw in your old self-talk and know the truth with which you need to replace it. Make yours a life of truth-seeking.

Argue. Maybe you were raised to think you shouldn't argue or fight. But wake up! When you're running on misbeliefs, you are on common ground with the father of lies, in concert with wicked, unseen principalities and powers. But you can fight back! (see Ephesians 6:10–18)

Practice. Memorize the truth you must repeat to yourself. Tape record it and listen to the tape over and over again. Most of all, *use it.* If you practice enough, you'll develop the positive habit of truthful self-talk.

What *Do* You Tell Yourself?

Tune in with me to several imaginary examples. These will not be dialogues between two persons, but between two natures *within* a person.

One voice is that of man's *old sinful nature* (OSN). This nature echoes the lies of the enemy and feeds into your mind misbelieving self-talk. The other voice is that of the *new nature* (NN). This nature is born of the Holy Spirit, and urges you to live by the truth that comes when you live in union with Him.

In each of the following three "dialogues," we will examine what can go on in the soul of a person who is facing a major adversity.

Here is background on a woman who has suffered an emotional loss—total rejection by her husband. Though the ensuing dialogue is created for purposes of illustration, Gwenn's story is, unfortunately, not uncommon.

Gwenn is a charming, intelligent, pretty mother of two preschoolers, who dedicated herself to home and family. She was crazy about her husband, Curt. But Curt began to change. He was harder and harder to please. Gwenn began to pray daily for Curt, but still he became unaffectionate and spent more time away from home. Suddenly, with no explanation, he moved out. Gwenn was stunned to learn that Curt had a male lover. She felt shattered.

Listen to Gwenn's "inner dialogue" a few days later:

New Nature (NN):	It's so hard to believe Curt is a homosexual. He was such a wonderful lover at first, so thoughtful and sensitive. But what am I going over all that for? I've got to think, figure out what to do, make some plans.
Old Sinful Nature (OSN):	You can't make *any* plans now. How can you even think of the future without Curt? Your life is as good as over.
NN:	No, that isn't true. I always feared losing Curt more than anything. And now that it's happened I'm hurting a lot—but I'm handling it! And I've still got my beautiful children. My life is *not* over. I still have God—
OSN:	God? What has He done for you lately? How can you

still believe God cares about you? Sure, the Bible says you are to be a submissive wife—but look how much you've lost by doing what the Bible says. You're being a fool. The Bible sounds good, but it doesn't work. Is the Bible going to support you? Feed your kids? Keep you warm in bed at night?

NN: I believe God answers prayer. Prayer has power.

OSN: You've *been* praying. Where has that gotten you? You ought to be angry! Tell God what you honestly think about Him. He let you be ripped off! How can He be God if He doesn't have the power to—

NN: Stop! Curt was not my whole life. I lived without him for twenty-two years before I ever met him. I have to confess that in many ways I turned Curt and my deep dependence on his love into idols. I am not hopeless, because I still have God on my side. And another thing, I'm not about to blame anybody for Curt's leaving. Least of all God. He *never* does wrong. Romans 9:14 says, "Is God unjust? Not at all!"

Curt's behavior is what's wrong—an affront to God and His commands. With his own free will, Curt chose to sin. The apostle James said, "God cannot be tempted by evil, nor does he tempt anyone; but each one is tempted when, by his own evil desire, he is dragged away and enticed."[2]

OSN: But, God could have *stopped* Curt from leaving you. Is God too weak and helpless to have kept you from this hurt? Or else He could have stopped you from marrying Curt in the first place.

NN: If He'd done that, I wouldn't have my children. And having them is worth this pain. Yes, it might have been easier all around if God had kept Curt out of my life—but I don't *know* that. I wanted to marry Curt, and I'm going to take the responsibility for

---

[2]James 1:13, 14.

the life I must live because of that decision. I know I'll make it through with God's help.

I believe the Bible when it says, "I consider that our present sufferings are not worth comparing with the glory that will be revealed in us."[3] The story isn't all written yet. I'm not giving up now. And God won't give up on me.

As you read this segment of inner dialogue, you might have noticed several things.

Our old sinful nature wants to push us back to the unbelieving state we were in before the new birth in Christ. In short, it wants to restore the *status quo* by putting itself back in charge. The reason is that the old nature is saturated with the sin power which, since Adam and Eve, has made unconverted human beings spiritually blind, dead and at enmity with God. The old nature is truly the enemy within, the part of us that Satan counts on to push his misbeliefs.

Second, the new nature loves and trusts God, even in difficulty. Therefore, it argues for God's truth.

Third, the new nature *can* vigorously debate against misbeliefs and replace them with the truth. We are perfectly capable of doing that when we have the Holy Spirit within.

Fourth, the new nature does not get defensive, but owns up to its responsibility for right choices. Unlike the old nature, the new nature refuses to get into the blame game.

The new nature also uses reason and concrete evidence to back its arguments. It uses Scripture to stop the old sinful nature's insinuations and false statements. The new nature knows that God cannot and will not lie— though the old nature always hints that He has lied to us.

Sixth, even when the new nature has gained a victory,

---

[3]Romans 8:18.

that doesn't mean the old sinful nature won't keep pushing misbeliefs. Similar skirmishes may need to be fought again.

We've seen, of course, that we can have rifts with God for many reasons. One reason, which we examined earlier, is our desire to have or do something God has told us is not good. We create some rifts by deciding to sin.

For instance, let's say your most besetting sin is *envy*. Envy is being sorry or unsettled when good happens to another person. If I'm envious, I'll be unhappy when a peer equals or surpasses me in some way I consider important. The envious preacher hopes his former classmate can't preach quite as well as he does. The envious suburbanite feels miserable because his neighbor has a better lawn mower or a new boat. The envious mother feels secret delight when her friend's son fails math. Suppose you and a close friend at work are up for the same promotion—and he gets it. You try to say the right things, but your envious thoughts and feelings bother you so much you can't work.

Let's tune in to the internal dialogue:

OSN: You know he gets all his good ideas from you. Why do you always open your big mouth?

NN: I refuse to cross over into an orgy of self-pity and envy. I've been there too many times, and it's too painful. I always end up depressed and mad at God over the whole thing. I *will* be thankful that he got the promotion.

OSN: On the other hand—isn't it possible that this Christian charity stuff can go too far? Pretty soon you'll be cheering everybody else on and shooting yourself in the foot! You don't have to be happy when they give a better job to someone who's inferior to you. It's a crime, and you're the victim. If God loves you, why would he let a dope beat you out of the job you prayed for? Can't you see it—God plays favorites.

You should be furious.

NN: No, God knows what He's doing with every one of His children. He knows what I need, and since I'm not omniscient I'm in no position to tell Him He's wrong. If He lets the job go to someone else I must side with His decision.

My job is to tell myself the truth: My gracious, kind, loving, wise Father wouldn't do wrong to me. He's one hundred percent faithful. So I'm hanging in there with Him. Even if I don't come out better in everything, what difference does that make? My Father has loaded me down with good things. I refuse to run away from God every time somebody does better than I. I will not send myself to the pits if somebody has something I don't have.

OSN: But what about those "promises" in the Bible? He didn't come through for you. That's the bottom line.

NN: No, it's not. Separation from God is the bottom line. God says envy is *not* good! "Rid yourselves of all malice and deceit, hypocrisy, envy and slander of every kind. Like newborn babies, crave pure spiritual milk, so that by it you may grow up in your salvation, now that you have tasted that the Lord is good."[4] Well, I've tasted. And to me He's all sweetness.

OSN: You're losing it. God just wants to crush out all your human strength. Make you weak. A nothing. You'll be walked all over by everyone. Be a *man*.

NN: I died to my old man in Christ Jesus. You're my worst enemy. The new me knows from experience how great I feel when I know God is for me and that everything will be fine if I stay close to Him. It's *terrific* that God has chosen to bless someone besides me. It's good for him—and for me, too.

Most of us need to win more than a few skir-

---

[4]1 Peter 2:1.

mishes before we claim victory over the sin of envy. But each time, our faith muscles grow stronger, until sin is conquered.

Triumph Over "Self"

Saints like Evagrius of Pontus, John Cassian, John of Damascus, and Thomas Aquinas (among other Christian writers from the fourth century on) referred to the sin of "sloth."[5] Today, we define sloth as laziness, but these early saints were referring to a state like depression, though they saw in it a deeper spiritual dimension.[6] They noted that the "slothful," or depressed person, avoided prayer and Bible reading, insisting spiritual pursuits were fruitless. They also described the depressive's feelings of dejection, restlessness, listlessness, mental exhaustion, belief that work is unbearable, and feeling that the days are too long. By calling it the *deadly sin* of sloth, they were asserting that at its core was a rift with God.

Here is a model dialogue illustrating how you may work at healing from depression. Remember, when you're depressed you don't feel like doing anything, particularly if it requires effort. The old sinful nature often takes that listlessness as its point of departure:

OSN: Why pick up this Bible? You don't get a thing out of it. It's not worth all the effort. Something is profoundly wrong with you, and nothing "spiritual"

---

[5]Their word was "sloth," one of the seven deadly sins. Read their descriptions, however, and you will discover that what they labeled "sloth" was the same state we call "depression." Noteworthy is the fact that they considered the condition one of the deadly *sins*, not a mere illness. John Cassian's (fourth century) description can be found cited in Wenzel, Siegried, *The Sin of Sloth*, "Acedia" in *Medieval Thought and Literature*, Chapel Hill, N.C.: University of North Carolina Press, 1967, p. 19.

[6]"*tristitia de bono spirituali*" —see *Summa Theologica* II-II, Q35, p. 58 in Aquinas, Thomas, *Aquinas Ethicus*: A translation of the principal portion of the second part of the "Summa Theologica" (tr. Joseph Rickoby), Vol. I & II. New York: Catholic Publication Society, 1892.

will help. When you read, the words run past your eyes in a blur. And don't try to pray, because you can't get through to God. Give up.

NN: It's true that I don't *feel* like doing anything. But it's a lie that I *can't*. Of course I *can*. My muscles aren't paralyzed, my eyes aren't glued shut, and my brain isn't dead. I won't buy the misbelief that since I don't *feel* energetic I have no energy. Or that there's no use praying when my prayers don't help me to feel God's presence. The Holy Spirit is giving me insight even though I don't feel good.

OSN: Why bring religion into this? It's meaningless, superstitious activity. Religion cannot cure your depression. You *are* depressed, and calling on God isn't going to make you feel better.

The truth is, you're not like that "religious" kind of person, anyway. You've never been able to feel it like those super-spiritual types who give their testimonies at church. You've always had doubts. Sure, you've buried them and acted the part, but deep down, you're the same old, meaningless, worthless you. Be honest and face the emptiness of life.

NN: Just because I don't feel good doesn't mean all is meaningless. God gave His Son's life on the cross for me. That gives life meaning. And whether He talks to me right now or not, His actions speak louder than words. His actions certify my value. He declares me significant, even when I'm not feeling energetic or valuable.

OSN: If God loves you so much, why doesn't He heal your depression? You're not getting better, and whose fault is that? God could help if He really wanted to. So where is He? Maybe He's too busy running the universe to pay attention to you. You don't *feel* as if He's listening, do you?

NN: No, I don't *feel* it. But I no longer go by my feelings.

They're temporary and changeable. I listen to God himself. Jesus was God, come to earth to tell us of His love. Jesus said, "Are not two sparrows sold for a penny? Yet not one of them will fall to the ground apart from the will of your Father. And even the very hairs of your head are all numbered. So don't be afraid; you are worth more than many sparrows."[7] I believe Him.

OSN: But those are just words. You're *still* depressed!

NN: Actually, the more I argue like this, the better I feel.

As for words—yours are lies. They come from the father of lies. The words of Jesus are the very words of God. And God's words are always impeccably true. "God, who does not lie, promised before the beginning of time, and at his appointed season he brought his word to light."[8]

Second, God is big enough to back up His words with actions. When Jesus Christ came and died and rose from death—that's *action*. "Surely the arm of the Lord is not too short to save, nor his ear too dull to hear."[9]

OSN: That *may* be true—but what about your doubts? You have to believe to be saved, and you're nothing but a jittery, demoralized bundle of doubts.

NN: That's not true, either. *For now* I have a mixture of beliefs in my mind. Some of them are strong, some weak, some even false. And there are doubts there, too. I'm not perfect—yet. But I'm growing in the truth given by the Holy Spirit. And right now I'm hanging on to the truth that Jesus Christ is my worth, my righteousness, my hope and my healer. I don't have to stay depressed, and I don't intend to.

Sure, it's hard to make myself get up and fight—

---

[7]Matthew 10:29.
[8]Titus 1:2.
[9]Isaiah 59:1.

but it's been good for me. I *am* going to read from God's Word.

The rift with God developed by the old sinful nature doesn't get very far in this dialogue. There are two reasons why. One is that the person, though depressed, deliberately fought against the lies of the devil fostered in the form of misbeliefs. The other is that the primary weapon wielded by the new nature was the Word of God.

You can learn to quote Scripture to yourself and to be virtually invincible. As you do this, you'll find that "'no weapon [misbelief] forged against you will prevail, and you will refute every tongue that accuses you. This is the heritage of the servants of the Lord, and this is their vindication from me, 'declares the Lord' " (Isaiah 54:17).

Develop the Art of Talking Back

Notice these points in the dialogues you've read:

First, your old nature has one objective: to open a rift between you and God. Only by succeeding can the OSN survive. Otherwise it is ultimately doomed.

Second, your old nature has a habit of using truth in a lying framework. So don't expect it never to cite any truth at all. It's the overall message you want to reject as a misbelief.

Third, your old nature has an odd existence. It *is* you, and it *isn't* you.

We have noticed in the clinic that when Christians take personality tests, the resulting profiles often describe their old sinful natures. This is because many of the questions concern the past. When we interpret these tests for them, they hear themselves described as angry, anxious, guilt ridden, fearful, avoiding others, behaving in hostile and threatening ways, suspicious, alienated or irritable. Sometimes these people are in a quandary because they don't see themselves that way anymore—yet they realize the picture is an accurate description of their old sinful nature.

If you're a Christian, you will always deal with one more nature than the unbeliever, because you have a new nature. Remember, though *you* are dead to the old sinful nature, *it* is most definitely not dead, and will attempt to recapture you for itself.

Fourth, your new nature can fight with a guarantee of victory, because God's Spirit of truth has become your ally and He cannot fail. But it won't always appear that way to you, because the old sinful nature twists and writhes in its attempt to hide that truth.

Lastly, the ultimate fabricator of all your misbeliefs is Satan, even if your old sinful nature won't admit it. You will be tempted to think your misbeliefs are based not on the devil's lies but on such good-sounding sources as "the facts," "what most people think," "results of scientific study," "psychologists' opinions," and "gut feelings." None of these is solid ground on which to stand, because none has ultimate truth. So challenge your old sinful nature when it bases a belief on any of its favorite *un*reliable sources. *Always* identify with your new nature.

The battle you're in *will* end. Not as soon as you would like it to, perhaps, but sooner than old sinful nature wants you to know. So fight the good fight!

But What If the Pain Keeps Coming Back?

You won't succeed if you expect to replace corrupt self-talk just one time and never have to do it again. The pain may return. And the misbeliefs on which your pain is based—being the weapons of a tireless Enemy—may reappear.

There is a resoluteness in these words of David: "I have set the Lord always before me. Because he is at my right hand, I will not be shaken" (Ps. 16:8). It's the resolve called for by Paul when he reminds us that we're in a battle, not the Rose Parade. What counts is the determination to stand and not be knocked down: "Finally, be strong in the Lord and in his mighty power. Put on the full armor of God so that you can take your stand against the devil's schemes . . . so that when the day of evil comes, you may be able to stand your ground, and after you have done everything, to stand. Stand firm then" (Ephesians 6:10–14).

"Set your mind." "Stand!" These are the words of Scripture. Stand and argue—again, and again, and again. You are in a battle with an Enemy who doesn't leave the field just because you've taken some action against him. Be prepared to insist on the truth within, to keep actively replacing lies with God's truth until the lies no longer percolate through your brain.

You can reach such a place. Unless you tell yourself the truth that God will not keep you in agony but will bring you through, you won't have the strength to persevere in the battle. But He *will* bring you through.

Whatever hurts now, there will come a time when it doesn't hurt anymore and won't ever hurt again!

Canoe Trip

FOREST FIRE

Along the shores, and up into the hills,
   stand blackened trunks of pines,
      stark relics of a forest fire;
And in among them, robust adolescent trees,
With just a few tall, stalwart sentinels,
   still thriving,
      thrusting their massive crowns
        into the sky.

They tell me that a forest fire,
   ravaging the brush and smaller trees,
      will leave these greater ones unscathed,
        breaking open tight-shut cones
        to bring to birth
        new life.

When you walk through fire
   you shall not be burned,
      and the flame shall not consume you.
For I am the Lord your God,
   the Holy One of Israel,
      your Saviour . . .
I am the Lord your God,
   who teaches you to profit.

ELEVEN

Sermons From Science

In the previous chapter, we learned about the art of talking back to the old sinful nature. As we saw, it's not enough to have truth planted in our heads. We must use it like a sword and fight for our lives. For, make no mistake, it is a struggle between life and death that we're talking about.

But—so many of us know that the spiritual war we're fighting is waged on slippery ground. Evil has many ways of looking attractive, while the good can look boring and unrewarding.

I believe there is one chief misbelief, very popular these days, that can undermine your spiritual stand. And I want to expose it for the lie it is. One of the most subtle misbeliefs you must learn to counter is this: "It doesn't matter if I go against God's commandments. My actions—good or bad—really have no consequences. I might as well give in and do whatever feels good."

The truth is: *Actions do have consequences.* God, who knows that you and I are motivated by rewards, built this dynamic into His system when He created us. So actions that go against Him have bad results for us. And actions in accordance with His will have good results for us. Remembering this, in the face of temptation, may be the only thing that makes you want to stand your ground when other forces try to persuade you to give in.

Because I believe it's so urgent that we keep ourselves aware of consequences, I want to take some time to examine an idea that may surprise you: Science verifies that living at peace with God—living the kind of life He wants us to live, in conformity with His laws—*is* the best way to live. Going against Him brings devastation.

And to introduce this idea, I must tell you about Marguerite, who had to stand her ground in the face of enormous pressure.

Standing Firm

Three weeks before her first visit to my office, Marguerite had left her job at a local hospital around 11:20 P.M. Walking to her car, she was suddenly overwhelmed with panic. Though she felt light-headed and weak, she managed to drive home. She couldn't imagine what was happening to her. She had been fearful and upset ever since.

We puzzled together over the cause of her anxiety. At last, at our third meeting, she whispered, "I have to tell you something, but I've been putting it off."

Reluctantly, her face flushed with embarrassment, she described how a friendship with a resident physician had snowballed into an affair. "I can't handle it. I don't want to give him up, but I can't leave my husband and my children. Going on like this is too terrible—I feel so awful, so guilty. I know it's wrong, but I don't know what to do."

I'm not trying to oversimplify the dynamics of Marguerite's neurosis, or to offer a universal explanation for all anxiety attacks. But for this woman, with her particular psychological makeup, panic symptoms were the consequence of the rift she had created with God by telling herself misbeliefs. As we worked together, Marguerite came to this conclusion herself.

"I've been kidding myself," she said. "Making myself believe that an affair was *good* for me because I didn't have enough love in my life. I've fed myself the idea that old morality is outmoded, that God can't possibly oppose such a beautiful thing as human love, that what I'm doing isn't hurting anybody and that I can keep it hidden.

"I see now that none of this is true. This affair has definitely *not* been good for me. In fact, it's made me sick—which is exactly what God's commandment predicted would happen. Though being with Don is exciting, most of the time I don't feel good. I feel terrible.

"Now I see the truth," she stated. "God loves me infinitely so He would never tell me anything harmful or deceptive. I'm going to rely on His Word and stop seeing Don. It won't be easy, because it *is* rewarding to be with someone who cares so much for me. But I don't want any more anxiety attacks. And more than that I don't want a gulf between me and my Father in heaven. Being reconciled with Him far outweighs whatever I'll lose when I give Don up.

"Even if I don't feel the good He's promised right away, I'm going to believe God and wait to enjoy the positive consequences He's promised to those who trust His truth!"

I was amazed at her determination—but not at all surprised by the difficult fight she had in trying to follow through.

As you might suspect, it wasn't easy for Marguerite to break off with Don "cold turkey." Once she did, though, he fought to overcome her resistance and pushed aggressively for dates. Then he became angry, calling her at home and sarcastically putting her down at work. He even threatened to tell her husband. Finally, he refused to speak to her unless hospital duties made interaction essential.

All this was painful, but Marguerite maintained her resolve by telling herself the truth: Her rift with God was healed. And her marriage, which she had counted dead on the vine, slowly grew tender and beautiful again. She was able to relax, free from nervous guilt. The panic attacks gradually receded into memory and were forgotten.

At our last session, Marguerite asked me if I would tell her story to others so you, too, could see that healing your rift with God brings unsurpassed rewards—the pearl of great price. You see, as Marguerite discovered, there is a lot of evidence that the best thing for you is to walk on God's side.

Now this is the interesting, scientific part. I'll summarize some research results that offer more truth about consequences. They can help you to continue walking with Him in truth when going against God appears to be the better way.

Research and the Rift With God

Does scientific research tell us that someone whose life is based on obedience to God actually *lives better* than someone who doesn't?

You might be surprised to learn that scientists have conducted studies on questions like this. They've looked into the consequences of sin in general, of drunk driving, of sex outside of marriage, of prayer for the sick, of serious Christian commitment, and more. And you might be even more surprised to learn that those who have overcome life's hurts and now live at peace with God do live better lives!

Study these remarkable examples, and remind yourself with them the next time your old nature tries to tell you disagreement with God has no consequences. Compared with the person who walks in falsehood and maintains a wide rift with God, the truthful person tends to be:

- more fulfilled, having more of his/her potential realized
- more tender-minded
- more conscientious
- more likely to have a purpose in life
- more aware of positive change in moods and emotions
- more concerned for other people
- more favorably inclined toward self, others and God

- more trusting
- more cooperative
- more self-controlled
- more tolerant
- more free of self-doubt
- more sociable
- more responsible
- more socially mature
- more capable of creating a favorable impression
- more achieving through conformity and intellectual efficiency
- more skilled at minimizing worries
- more likely to enjoy marital happiness
- more skilled at family problem-solving
- more healthy in sexuality
- more healthy in mind and in spirit because they have a good prayer life
- more physically healthy (lower blood pressure, less heart disease, higher cancer survival rates)
- more likely to live longer and to fear death less[1]
- less guilt-prone and anxious
- less likely to engage in risky, life-threatening behavior
- less wrapped up in money, prestige and materialistic goals
- less neurotic
- less likely to suffer marital failure
- less likely to have delinquent offspring
- less likely to be trapped in drug or alcohol abuse
- less likely to abuse narcotics
- less likely to use tobacco

---

[1]For readers who would like to examine this research in more detail, documentation is included in the Appendix.

• less likely, as adolescents, to drink alcohol[2]

Yes, science affirms that those who pray and trust God to answer prayer live healthier lives. Prayer is, of course, our mental/spiritual bridge to God. If that bridge is knocked apart by angry, doubtful thoughts, you and I fall into the abyss of living away from God.

Is it any wonder that one of the truths most commonly attacked is the truth about prayer? Perhaps you've heard yourself saying or thinking something like this: "You can't get anywhere by praying. God probably won't answer anyway. Just think of all the sick people who would be well and strong right now if prayer really worked! Forget God. You've got to help yourself because no one else will help you."

If that's what's in your self-talk, it contradicts the love of God, and that's the very keystone in the bridge we must build across every rift. *"God is love"*—that is the main support over every abysmal circumstance (see 1 John 4:8).

On the specific matter of prayer, the Scriptures give us many firm assurances that God does hear and answer prayer. Here is a sampling:

Psalm 6:9: The Lord has heard my cry for mercy; the Lord accepts my prayer.

Psalm 55:16: I call to God, and the Lord saves me.

Jeremiah 33:3: The Father says, "Call to me and I will answer you and tell you great and unsearchable things you do not know."

Matthew 7:7, 8: Jesus says, "Ask . . . seek . . . knock. For everyone who asks receives; he who

---

[2]Dr. William Wilson, a distinguished psychiatric researcher, graciously provided a bibliography on religion and health which is reprinted in the Appendix. Some of these findings, taken from his work, document positive outcomes attributable in part to dietary habits common among Seventh-day Adventists. Since these are based on Old Testament Law, a gift of God to His people of long ago, these results are additional evidence of the blessings stemming from a solid, peaceful relationship with God.

seeks finds; and to him who knocks, the door will be opened."

John 14:14: Jesus says, "You may ask me for anything in my name, and I will do it."[3]

A particularly well-designed experiment recently confirmed the biblical promise that intercessory prayer for the sick has powerful consequences. Because it provides such a near-perfect example of exemplary research methodology, its findings are even more striking than individual case histories.

This fascinating research by Dr. Randolph C. Byrd[4] demonstrated that patients in a coronary care unit who were prayed for showed better and faster improvement than those given medical treatment only and without prayer. These results were *not* attributable to the power of suggestion or to accidental factors. Dr. Byrd's report, in a recent issue of the *Southern Medical Journal,* was eye-opening.

Two identical groups of patients were involved in the experiment. Each member of one group was prayed for daily by name by a Christian who believed strongly that God wants to heal. Members of the other group were not prayed for during the experiment. Each volunteer prayed for one patient, and they prayed at home so that no one in the hospital, including the patients themselves, knew which patients were in the prayed-for group and which were not. This provision was considered especially impor-

---

[3]Here is a list of more passages documenting God's guarantee that He will answer prayers which are according to His will and made by a person who is in a peaceful relationship with Him: Psalm 5:3, 65:2–5, 66:19, 86:6–7, 91:15, 102:17; Proverbs 15:8 and 29; Isaiah 30:19, 58:9, 65:24; Jeremiah 29:12; Joel 2:19; Matthew 6:5–6, 7:11, 18:19, 21:22; Mark 11:24, 14:38–39; John 1:7 and 16, 16:23, 24, 26; Romans 12:12; 1 Thessalonians 5:17, 1 Timothy 2:8; James 1:5–6, 4:2–3, 5:13–16; 1 John 3:22, 5:14–16. Why not memorize any or all of these truthful and reliable words if you find that they speak to you?

[4]Cardiology Division, San Francisco General Medical Center, and the Department of Medicine, University of California, San Francisco.

tant to avoid any possibility of ascribing results to the power of suggestion.[5]

The results: Those who were prayed for required less assistance with breathing, also fewer antibiotics and diuretics. They also showed less significant severity than the other group after the daily prayers began and during their entire hospital stay. The groups were measured before the experiment and found to have identical needs in all these respects at the outset. So the only reason for the differences between the groups was prayer.

These results constitute solid evidence that the prayers of a man or woman who is walking in the truth have great effect.

Some Negative Consequences of Living by Misbeliefs

Sometimes our misbeliefs tempt us. They sound so plausible, urging us to see ourselves as abused by God, or perhaps as deprived of the "fun" we think others are having in their disobedience. "God and His laws are not good" is the bottom line of this radical misbelief.

Put that way, it sounds so silly most of us would reject it. But our old nature hardly ever phrases its message quite that way. Instead, misbeliefs may take the guise of insinuations: "The Ten Commandments are old and out-of-date. They're no longer pertinent or even true. All they

---

[5]For readers interested in experimental design, Dr. Byrd used a prospective randomized double-blind protocol with a treatment group of 192 subjects and a control group of 201 subjects. No differences were found between the groups at the beginning of treatment, but the treatment group had a significantly lower severity score during their hospital course ($p < .01$). Multivariant analysis separated the groups on the basis of the outcome variables ($p < .0001$). The control patients required ventilatory assistance, antibiotics and diuretics more frequently than patients in the treatment group. Incidentally, since it was obviously not possible for Dr. Byrd to be certain that friends and relatives weren't praying for at least some of the patients in the control group, we can assume the results are less spectacular then they would be if members of the control group had absolutely no one praying for them.

do is prevent us from expressing ourselves fully. True freedom comes from giving free rein to every desire. God doesn't want to limit us."

But the truth is, God and His Word are the only reliable guides to good. The "trends" in society have little to offer, really, in terms of well-being.

One example for which we have empirical evidence is alcohol abuse. Though God has forbidden it, many people equate getting drunk with celebrating, forgetting their troubles, or enjoying themselves. The National Center for Disease Control has released carefully analyzed data on the results of alcohol abuse, demonstrating that most automobile crashes (85 percent) involve at least one driver who is drunk. Nearly half of all fatally injured adult pedestrians are drunk when they're hit.

Another popular disagreement with God is over sinful sex. Writers and TV and movie producers have made fun of God's truth about sexual morality. People who proudly substitute their own conclusions for those revealed by God have assured us there is nowadays nothing to fear in disobeying the ancient rules. So a large segment of the population has put the "new morality" to the test.

The results have been expensive in terms of ruined lives. One of our greatest social problems is teenage pregnancy; another is welfare-supported, single-parent homes. Not only does abortion claim thousands of unborn lives each day, it has torn apart the fabric of our society. Doctors are treating an epidemic number of people, young and old, for sexually transmitted diseases ranging from syphilis, to genital warts, to AIDS.

I'll mention only one striking finding of research conducted in this area of sexual behavior. According to a study released by the National Bureau of Economic Research, couples who live together before marriage have an eighty percent *higher* divorce rate than those who do not. The authors of the study caution against inferring that living together before marriage *causes* divorce. It may be that both living together and divorce are caused by believing the same misbeliefs: that it's good to do whatever you want, without limitation. In any case, the result is still shattered relationships, emotional pain, financial crippling—and very, very little good.

When Your Foot Is Slipping

Suppose you're flagging in your war against misbeliefs—becoming angry at God, doubting that what He has revealed about the good can actually work. Suppose you start to feel that it's easier to drift away from God than to battle the storm. Let's tune in to some sample self-talk:

OSN: Look at the way God treats you, after you've tried so hard to be faithful. Maybe in your case there *won't* be any good consequences from all your hard work. How long do you think you can keep up such a super-human effort? You aren't getting anywhere "telling yourself the truth about the good." What you're trying to do doesn't pay! Give up and give in. You're a fool to try so hard when other people are getting away with it every day.

This is the time to tell yourself the truth about consequences. Your new nature can say something like this:

NN: This is all authored by the father of lies. God's Word describes consequences on nearly every page: "Those who fear Him lack nothing. The lions may grow weak and hungry, but those who seek the Lord lack no good thing" [Psalm 34:9, 10]. I know turning from God looks attractive at this point. But I've seen pretty clearly the bad consequences of relying on your own ideas about what's good, rather than staying close to God. No, I'm sticking with Him. He loves me and He'll see me through this time of trouble and temptation. It won't last forever.

Perhaps you've even come to this point of temptation before, only to cross over the line into disagreement with God. Maybe you've tried to tell yourself the truth. Maybe you've argued with your old sinful nature—and still decided to turn away from God, even just momentarily, to do the thing that seems good and appealing. Then you feel like a dog, slinking back to its master with its tail between its legs.

I want to let you in on one more secret weapon of the old sinful nature, one more misbelief it will use to try to separate you from God. It is this: "It's awful and embarrassing to let God know you're attracted by sin. So don't tell Him when you're being tempted. Hide it from Him. He wants all His children to be strong—so what will He think of you if He finds out how weak you really are? What will He think if He knows how attractive sin looks to you?"

In case you're not aware of this fact, God *already* knows all your weaknesses. He already knows what tempts you. And He's not shocked, dismayed or offended by that knowledge. As David put it, "He knows how we are formed, he remembers that we are dust" (Psalm 103:14).

When you're tempted to disagree with God and make the first step away from Him, I recommend that this is the precise moment you should turn *to* Him and say, "Lord, you see that I'm being tempted. You see where the enemy is overwhelming me with misbeliefs. I need you to help me keep my eyes on you, because I've almost lost sight of you in this battle."

God tells us what His sure response will be when one of His own calls out to Him from the thick of a spiritual fray: "Call upon me in the day of trouble and I will deliver you, and you will honor me" (Psalm 50:15).

That's right, at the very moment you're tempted, hurt, angry, feeling spiritually cold, *call upon God.* We who are Christians say that salvation comes as a graceful gift of God. But we forget that salvation is more than being saved from hell. God wants to save you and me from every heartache we would bring upon ourselves by saying we're His, but living as if we're not His. And David, who went through many troubles that were his own making as well as those that evil men tried to bring upon him, took command of his own soul, saying: "I will sing of your strength, in the morning I will sing of your love; for you are my fortress, my refuge in times of trouble" (Psalm 59:16).

I can also promise you, from my own experience and the reports of countless others, that if you turn to God at the very moment that voice inside of you tells you to run from Him, He will stretch forth His hand of love and grip you tightly so you will not fall away.

For the truth about God is that He is not like us. His ego is not damaged at the first whiff that you and I disagree with Him. He doesn't push us away when we're weak and, with bitterness say, "If you think you know so much, go ahead and do it your way. But you'll see!"

He only wants truth and honesty—all the time, in all circumstances. Spiritual cover-ups don't do anything but keep us further from Him. So the next time you feel yourself slipping away from God and embarrassed to let Him know it, consider this passage, written by the apostle John:

> If we claim to be without sin, we deceive our-selves and the truth is not in us. If we confess our sins, he is faithful and just and will forgive us our sins and purify us from all unrighteousness. (1 John 1:8, 9)

Here is a prayer I highly recommend you keep in your spiritual arsenal for weak moments:

> Lord, you know what I'm thinking right now. You know what it is I want to do that's against you. I'm not going to keep up a false front with you—I con-fess that a big part of me wants to go my own way. This is the point of my weakness. This is my front line of battle, and my old nature is trying to drag

me away and make me a captive again. But I don't want to turn away from you and live according to lies. Help me right now by surrounding me with your Spirit like a fortress of truth. Make the truth so strong in my mind and my spirit that I not only think it but I *do* it. I know that you are in me, and that you are greater than any force in this world.

Canoe Trip

RESTORATION

Delicate wilderness,
You too have once been ravaged
    by the cruel axe,
Yet now you beckon us to bowered splendour,
Feasting us from diamond-studded waters,
Laying us to rest on couches
    pillowed with the finest of green moss,
And calling us to worship in cathedrals
    solemn with the music
        of the wind.

*And the Lord restored
    the fortunes of Job.*

TWELVE

The Healed Rift

Perhaps you've read other "self-help" books—each of which has advocated a way of life, suggested changes or, at least, promoted new insights. Each is based on the assumption that you can make things better by trying its program. Perhaps you're wondering if the suggestions offered in *this* book will bring results that are worth the effort.

I've tried to answer this question in two ways: (1) by showing you what the Bible says about the outcomes; (2) by assembling research results—both of which demonstrate that, yes, getting back on God's side does work.

One more line of evidence is my own personal experience. I have shared with you how my own rift with God occurred and widened, as well as how it was healed. Now I want to tell you one more story from my own experience. I think it will furnish an example of how agreeing with God, even in the midst of catastrophe, makes all the difference.

The Explosion

On November 21, 1985, I was standing in front of our furnace with the firebox door wide open, peering inside. I'd come home that evening to find Candy trying to balance a checkbook but hardly able to think because she'd been inhaling fumes from our oil-burning furnace. I realized from the odor permeating the house that the problem was incomplete combustion.

This problem had occurred before and I'd been able to

take care of it. So I ran down the stairs, opened the firebox door and saw immediately what was amiss. A half inch of carbon had built up on the injector nozzle through which pressurized oil is squirted into the combustion chamber. Some of the oil hadn't burned, so it lay in a pool on the floor of the chamber. I did what I'd done before. Grabbing a metal tool, I chipped the carbon from the nozzle. It fell off all right—but a bit of it was red hot. When that glowing cinder touched the pool of volatile heating oil, the resulting explosion blew the front and back out of the furnace and shot flaming oil all over my arms, face and head.

I was a living torch.

I ran from the furnace room and rolled on the carpet to put out the flames. *I'm going to die,* I thought. And at that same moment, I felt a sense of calm I can't quite believe even now. Meanwhile Candy had heard the explosion and run downstairs, wondering if she would find me alive or dead. When she found me the flames were extinguished and I was still conscious and breathing normally. (I later learned that sometimes in this kind of accident, the trachea swells so you can't breathe.) When she saw me, she called upon her training as a former flight attendant. "Get into the shower! Turn on the cold water, and spray it on your face and hands!"

Somehow, I was able to get to my feet and stumble to the shower. As cold water ran over my body, I noticed shreds of skin hanging from my face and the backs of my hands.

It was in the shower that I suddenly became aware of something: I was worshiping God aloud! It sounded awfully noisy and a little peculiar. Why was I singing at a time like this? I wondered if I'd slipped over the edge mentally. Loud and clear, the praise kept pouring out of my mouth, even though I realized I didn't know whether I would live or die.

Candy, for her part, had punched the emergency phone number, 911, and firemen and paramedics were on their way. With black smoke filling the basement, I crawled up the stairs. I lay on the floor by the front door where, even though I was going into shock, I spent the next quarter hour shaking—and praising God! (By now *Candy* was wondering what was happening to me mentally . . .)

I was eventually taken to the world-renowned burn unit at Ramsey County Hospital in St. Paul. There I was "boiled" in a huge vat of scalding hot water with clorox, then treated by a wonderful nurse who somehow managed to convey love and at the same time inflict searing pain as she scrubbed away shreds of blackened skin. I'm sure the morphine helped. And still, my heart was filled with the praises of God. By now, of course, I could hardly believe I was doing this—but I wasn't about to make it stop.

After the scraping and bandaging, they gave me a comfortable bed beside a great, wide window that looked out on the downtown district.

Once Candy was assured I was going to make it, she was urged to go to the home of a friend and rest. I was alone and vibrantly awake. Outside my window, the city of St. Paul had long before fallen asleep. The moon, large in the wintry sky, illuminated the beauty spread out before me. I didn't sleep that night, but lay there looking out the window at the lights and, as morning drew near, the increasing traffic on the freeway. No one could tell how much of my face and hands would emerge from the bandages intact, or whether I would need skin grafts. Yet . . . all the time, I kept praising the God and Father of my Lord Jesus Christ for His kindness.

Through the long months of my convalescence, there were many more sessions of "boiling and scraping." The bandages I wore for weeks and then the compression gloves prescribed to prevent scarring tore loose the scabs, exposing raw flesh every single morning. It was a time of severe restriction on my activities because I couldn't expose my skin to sun or sub-zero weather—a real problem in Minnesota! Though I felt pain as I'd never known before,

I knew and remembered *God is good.*

The physicians expected me to develop a depression which, evidently, is par for the course when one's severely burned. But I didn't. Instead—and this is the mystery—just at those times when the pain rose to its screaming zenith, I felt close to God.

Even then I wondered why my reaction was so totally different from my long-ago response to the divorce. How could the man who in one set of negative circumstances blamed and cursed God praise Him in another? As you can see, something had changed.

Between the night years ago when I drove home yelling at God and the night more recently when I lay in the hospital, uncertain how much of my face I would ever see again, there had come an inner transformation. And it had taken place because God had revealed His truth in a new way.

Instead of turning from God and looking back over my shoulder only to accuse and blaspheme, I was able to learn new truth from my pain. I learned, for example, how to draw nearer to God in catastrophe rather than opening up a rift with Him. I learned how to place everything in God's hands, regardless of what the circumstances look like, because He knows how to bestow what is good. I was able to tell myself of the absolute reliability of God's promise: "When you walk through the fire, you will not be burned; the flames will not set you ablaze. For I am the Lord, your God, the Holy One of Israel, your Savior" (Isaiah 43:2, 3). To me, this passage was God's guarantee that even if some of my flesh was destroyed, no conflagration could ever touch my real self, my soul.

If you refuse to pull away from God, tragedy and temptation can actually draw you to a fuller knowledge of the truth than you've ever had before: *Nothing* can separate you from the love of God that is in Christ Jesus.

Here are some truths pain and loss can teach:

The truth of God's real presence. The Sunday before

the explosion, I had concluded a course I'd been teaching, an exposition of the book of Job. Although we found tremendous wisdom in the book, I had to confess to my students, "I don't think I really grasp what this book is saying."

During our ten weeks of study two persons in the class died, while several others suffered major life upheavals. After the course was over, I was burned. *Then*, I understood about Job—how you must sometimes go through pain to come to the pinnacle, the most exalted experience of life. Not until the end of Job's book—after he has experienced loss, pain and the sense that God has rejected him—does Job become aware of the purpose of it all: "My ears had heard of you *but now my eyes have seen you*" (Job 42:5). Seeing, knowing, touching, experiencing, sensing, *encountering* God—that was God's end purpose for Job's suffering.

Once, after a terribly painful session of scraping and scrubbing, I was in such agony that the bed shook with my trembling. Candy stood there, hurting for me, asking how she could help. I could only reply, truthfully, "I'm touching the throne of God right now. Don't feel sorry for me."

It is true, and someone needs to affirm it: In the midst of every anguish, you can know God's wondrous presence as at no other time—if you know the truth and engrave it on your heart.

Second, pain and loss can teach you the truth that you can hack it. One of my old misbeliefs was, "I couldn't stand it if anything really terrible happened to me. I can't stand pain." Perhaps you, too, believe secretly that you're a fragile, flimsy creature, much too frail to survive a major loss or agony. So you tell yourself how dreadful such a thing would be, how it would utterly destroy you.

If you have never read the opening passages of Job I urge you to do so. There we learn that God sets definite limits for Satan. If you fear overly much that you couldn't stand pain, that it would vaporize you, maybe you can learn from my experience. I thought the same thing once. But now I know it's not so. God sets limits on what the "flames" of adversity can do. They can, as one hymn puts it, "consume your dross" and "refine your gold," but they can't actually do you real harm. You *can* survive it.

Third, you can learn the truth that the outcome will be good. I had a misbelief, years ago, that things would always go from bad to worse. If evil A happens to you, then evil B will follow, after which evil C will occur, and that will bring about evil D. Evil D will be *so* bad nothing could be worse. How silly that pessimism seemed when, recently, I interviewed a young Christian who had an advanced case of AIDS.

We were at a conference and the interview was conducted on stage, in public, for the instruction of the participants. In the course of one of his responses, Joe said something I'll never forget: "I wouldn't trade what AIDS has taught me for perfect health, even if I could." He said this, knowing of course that his illness would soon end his young life. For him, the good he'd gained made the bad worthwhile.

What Made the Difference?

My concern is that you will read this chapter and say, "Well, bully for you! It's nice that you could come out so well. But I'm not as fortunate as you, and all your story does to me is increase my sense of alienation and agony!" Or perhaps you'll say, "My sins are too important to me. I can't afford to give them up. So, to me your story sounds like Goody-Two-Shoes. You just don't understand me."

You may be right—but only partly right. Yes, your tragedy may be worse than anything I've ever known. Your sins may seem vital to your life.

If you won't believe *me*, believe God. He says that no tragedy is so great that His truth isn't greater:

> Therefore we do not lose heart. Though outwardly we are wasting away, yet inwardly we are being renewed day by day. For our light and momentary troubles are achieving for us an eternal glory that far outweighs them all. So we fix our eyes not on what is seen, but on what is unseen. For what is seen is temporary, but what is unseen is eternal. (2 Corinthians 4:16–18)

And no sin, no matter how important, can be worth the loss of your soul. Jesus said,

> Do not be afraid of those who kill the body but cannot kill the soul. Rather, be afraid of the One who can destroy both soul and body in hell. (Matthew 10:28)

You, too, can have God's truth so alive in you, starting now, that you find harmony and peace with God no matter what befalls you. Your rift can be healed. That's what made the difference for me. It's what makes the hope-filled difference one day, one step at a time—for people like Irene Gifford, whose story appeared in the beginning of this book. From the bleakest experience, from the furthest side of the rift with God, we can be brought close to Him again as His friends, with nothing separating us, not even the bitterness of sin or death (see Colossians 1:21–23). It is an inner transformation we need, as Irene so poetically portrays it:

MORNING GLORIES

Hard, black seed
   in a dying husk,
Cast upon the earth
   when it was winter.
How could you enclose such life,

and burst your shell
to live again?

Vibrant green vines,
spreading your arms
in exuberant dance,
twining together,
reaching and thrusting,
over and through
gardens and fences,
Profusion of praise.

Brilliant trumpets,
opening wide
to give
and to receive.
You are to me
a parable
of Resurrection.

For the trumpet shall sound,
and the dead shall be raised
Imperishable,
And we shall be changed. . . .

This transformation begins as God's truth takes root
and bears its fruit in you. Take a moment right now and
pray. I hope you will mean it *with all your heart*:

Lord, heal the rift my misbeliefs and sins have
created. Send your Spirit to work the truth into my
heart. Shine your light on my arguments with you
over the good. Touch my will that I may agree with
you and by the gift of faith, I want to be brought
into harmony and fellowship with you. Through
Jesus Christ, my Savior. Amen.

APPENDIX

A Bibliography on Religion and Health

Barton, Keith and G. M. Vaughan. "Church Membership and Personality: A Longitudinal Study." *Social Behavior & Personality.* 1976, Vol. 4 (1), 11–16.

Bolt, Martin. "Purpose in Life and Religious Orientation." *Journal of Psychology & Theology.* 1975 (Spring), Vol. 3 (2), 116–118.

Burke, Joseph F. "The Relationship Between Religious Orientation and Self-Actualization Among Selected Catholic Religious Groups." *Dissertation Abstracts.* 1973 (Oct.), Vol. 34 (4–B), 1721–1722.

Coates, Thomas J. "Personality Correlates of Religious Commitment: A Further Verification." *Journal of Social Psychology.* 1973 (Feb.), Vol. 89 (1), 159–160.

Cohen, Eric J. "Holiness and Health: An Examination of the Relationship Between Christian Holiness and Mental Health." *Journal of Psychology and Theology.* 1977 (Fall), Vol. 5 (4), 285–291.

Hamby, June. "Some Personality Correlates of Four Religious Orientations." *Dissertation Abstracts.* 1973 (Sept.), Vol. 34 (3–A), 1127–1128.

Nelson, Franklyn L. "Religiosity and Self-Destructive Crises in the Institutionalized Elderly." *Suicide & Life-Threatening Behavior.* 1977 (Summer), Vol. 7 (2), 67–74.

Spilka, Bernard. "Utilitarianism and Personal Faith." *Journal of Psychology and Theology.* 1977 (Summer), Vol. 5 (3), 226–233.

Spilka, Bernard and Michael Mullin. "Personal Religion and Psychological Schemata: A Research Approach to a Theological Psycholog_ of Religion." *Character Potential.* 1977 (Aug), Vol. 8 (2), 57–66.

Stanley, Gordon and Peter Vagg. "Attitude and Personality Characteristics of Australian Protestant Fundamentalists." *Journal of Social Psychology.* 1975 (Aug.), Vol. 96 (2), 291–292.

Wilson, William P. "Mental Health Benefits of Religious Salvation." *Diseases of the Nervous System.* 1972 (June), Vol. 33 (6), 382–386.

Attitudes:

The Connecticut Mutual Life Report on American Values in the 80's: The Impact of Belief. Hartford: Connecticut Mutual Life Ins. Co., 1981.

Data on Marital Status and Success:

Larson, D. B. "Religious Involvement, its Association with Marital Status, Marital Well Being and Morality." *Family Building.* George Rekers, ed.

190

Ventura, Calif.: Regal Books, 1985.

Landis, J. T. and Landis, M. G. *Building a Successful Marriage*, 7th ed. Englewood Cliffs, N.J.: Prentice-Hall, 1977.

Crisis in the Family:

Wilson, W. P. "Problem Solving in Crises." *Family Building*. George Rekers, ed. Ventura, Calif.: Regal Books, 1985.

Religion and Sexuality:

Tauris, C. and S. Sadd. *The Redbook Report on Female Sexuality*. New York: Delacorte Press, 1977.

Mentally Healthy and Unhealthy Children:

Glueck, S. and E. Glueck. *Delinquents and Nondelinquents in Perspective*. Cambridge, Mass.: Harvard University Press, 1968.

Grinker, R. R. Sr., R. R. Grinker Jr., and J. Imberlake. "Mentally Healthy Young Males (Homoclites)." *Arch. Gen. Psychiatry*. 6:405–453, 1962.

Wilson, W. P. *Christian Nurture and the Development of Mental Disease*. The Finch Lectures, Fuller Theological Seminary, Pasadena, Calif.: Unpublished.

Kalter, N. "Children of Divorce in Outpatient Psychiatric Population." *American Journal of Orthopsychiatry*. 47:4–51, 1977.

Effect of Faith on Mental Health of Adults:

Wilson, W. P. "Mental Health Benefits of Religious Salvation." *Dis. of the Nerv. System*. 33:382–386, 1972.

Religion and Physical Health:

Comstock, G. W. and K. B. Partridge. "Church Attendance and Health." *Journal of Chronic Disorders*. 25:665–672, 1972.

Byrne, J. T. and J. H. Rice. "In Sickness and in Health: The Effects of Religion." *Health Education*. 10:6–10, 1979.

Tuberculosis:

Kemmerer, J. M. and G. W. Comstock. "Sociologic Concomitants of Tuberculin Sensitivity." *American Review of Respiratory Diseases*. 96:885–892.

Blood Pressure:

Graham, T. W., B. H. Kaplan, J. C. Cornoni-Huntley, S. A. James, C. Becker, C. G. Hames, and S. Heyden. "Frequency of Church Attendance and Blood Pressure Elevation." *Behavioral Medicine*. 1:37–43, 1978.

Rouse, I. L., B. K. Armstrong, and L. J. Beilin. "The Relationship of Blood Pressure to Diet and Lifestyle in Two Religious Populations." *Journal of Hypertension*. 1:65–71, 1983.

Heart Disease:

Phillips, R. L., F. R. Lemon, W. L. Beeson, and J. W. Kuzma. "Coronary Heart Disease Mortality Among Seventh-day Adventists with Differing Dietary Habits: A Preliminary Report." *American Journal of Clinical Nutrition.* 31 (10 Supp):S191–S198, 1978.

Drugs and Alcohol:

Adlaf, E. M. and R. G. Smart. "Drug Use and Religious Affiliation." *British Journal of Addiction.* 80:163–171, 1985.

Larson, D. B. and W. P. Wilson. "Religious Life of Alcoholics." *Southern Medical Journal.* 73:723–727, 1980.

Cancellero, L. A., D. B. Larson, and W. P. Wilson. "Religious Life of Narcotic Addicts."*Southern Medical Journal.* 75:1166–1168, 1982.

Burkett, S. R. "Religiosity, Beliefs, Normative Standards and Adolescent Drinking." *Journal Stud. Alcohol.* 41:662–671, 1980.

Westermeyer, J. and V. Walzer. "Drug Usage: An Alternative to Religion." *Disorders of the Nervous System.* 36:492–495, 1975.

Cancer:

Zollinger, T. W., R. L. Phillips, and J. W. Kuzma. "Breast Cancer Survival Rates among Seventh Day Adventists and Non-Seventh Day Adventists." *American Journal of Epidemiology.* 119:503–509, 1984.

Lemon, F. R., R. T. Walden, and R. W. Woods. "Cancer of the Lung and Mouth in Seventh Day Adventists." *Cancer.* 17:486–497, 1964.

Tobacco Usage:

Hay, D. R. and F. H. Foster. "The Influence of Race, Religion, Occupation and other Social Factors on Cigarette Smoking in New Zealand." *International Journal of Epidemiology.* 10:41–43, 1981.

Morbidity and Mortality:

Le Riche. "Age at Death: Physicians and Ministers of Religion." *Canadian Medical Journal* 133:107, 1985.

Jarvis, G. K. and H. C. Northcott. "Religion and Differences in Morbidity and Mortality." *Soc. Sci. Medicine.* 25:813–824, 1987.

Death and Fear of Death:

Smith, D. K., A. M. Nehemkis, and R. A. Charter. "Fear of Death, Death Attitudes and Religious Conviction in the Terminally Ill." *International Journal of Psychiatry and Medicine.* 13:221–232, 1983–84.

Please note: This list of source articles is not complete and not up to date. It must be noted that some researchers have failed to find the positive consequences appearing in most of the work done using Allport's or Spilka's techniques. On the whole, I believe I have fairly characterized (though in a simplified form) the available findings.